The Invisible Land

A Study of the Artistic Imagination
of Iurii Olesha

THE INVISIBLE LAND

A Study of the Artistic Imagination of Iurii Olesha

ELIZABETH KLOSTY BEAUJOUR

Columbia University Press
NEW YORK AND LONDON
1970

Library of Congress Catalog Card Number: 71-130959
ISBN: 0-231-03428-8
Printed in the United States of America

FOR MY PARENTS

Acknowledgments

I should like to thank Professors William Harkins, Robert Maguire, and Richard Gustafson for their expert advice during the preparation of the original version of this book which was submitted as a Columbia University Ph.D. dissertation.

My debt to Rufus Mathewson and Robert Belknap is for much more than their help with my work on Olesha. I am also deeply grateful to them for continuing patience, encouragement, and cheer.

The following firms have kindly given me permission to quote from their books: Editions Gallimard for *A la Recherche du temps perdu;* Meridian Books for translations of Maiakovskii's poetry which they published in *The Bedbug and Selected Poetry*, edited by Patricia Blake and translated by George Reavey; *Opyty* for part of an article by Petr Ershov: "Odesskaia literaturnaia kolybel' ".

New York, 1968 E. K. B.

Contents

The Invisible Land

A Study of the Artistic Imagination
of Iurii Olesha

Fancy is the beloved of reason.

IURII OLESHA

Multiplier les formes par elles-mêmes,
ce n'est pas produire l'être.

GUSTAVE FLAUBERT

"Art Embraces My Life like the Sky"[1]

Iurii Karlovich Olesha was young with the century. Born in Elizavetgrad in 1899, he grew up in the cosmopolitan atmosphere of Odessa. The family was of Polish extraction, and later Olesha jestingly attributed his inability to write a whole Russian sentence in a single sweep to the fact that his first language was Polish.[2] His father, a former landowner, was an excise-tax official, and despite a dark family legend that Karl Antonovich had lost all his money at cards, the Oleshas lived a relatively comfortable bourgeois existence.

Although Olesha has recorded the small, private events of childhood which were of continuing importance to him throughout his life, he has said almost nothing of his experiences during the 1917 Revolution and the ensuing civil war. Once, in his "autobiographical novel" *No Day without a Line* [*Ni dnia bez strochki*], he does mention serving with an artillery battery near Odessa, but that fact is almost incidental to the main subject of the paragraphs which describe a school friend's visit and the virile charm of the sailors manning the battery.[3]

The tour of active duty was relatively brief, for during most of the Revolution and civil war Olesha's major activity was his participation in The Green Lamp [Zelenaia lampa], a young poets' club proudly named after the club to which Pushkin

[1] Iurii Olesha, "Koe-chto iz sekretnykh zapisei poputchika Zanda," *30 dnei*, No. 1 (1932), p. 15.

[2] Olesha, *Ni dnia bez strochki*, p. 43.

[3] *Ibid.*, pp. 131-32.

had belonged. In the critical year 1918, The Green Lamp published an almanac in which there was not one poem about the Revolution.[4] Eduard Bagritskii, Valentin Kataev, Zinaida Shishova, and Semen Kirsanov also belonged to the group, which gathered every day to talk of literary matters, dream of Moscow, read and vigorously criticize one another's works.[5]

During this period, Olesha, already a meticulous craftsman, had set himself the considerable task of writing a cycle of poems on Pushkin's themes. In his interesting memoir,[6] Petr Ershov has recorded his recollection of part of Olesha's "Queen of Spades" ["Pikovaia dama"]. It is one of the few fragments of Olesha's early verse still accessible to Western readers:

Shvyrnul shinel'. Voshel uprugo.
Blestia v parkete. Igroki.
Zatianuty zatylki tugo
V galunnye vorotniki.
Idet. Sluga skloniaet plechi,
V chulkakh i belom parike.
Sherenga slug stoit, i svechi
Koptiat amurov v potolke.
—Zdorovo, Germann!—On poklona
Ne zamechaet, podoshel
I profilem Napoleona
Sklonilsia i gliadit na stol . . .

[He flings down his coat, enters with elastic step.
The reflection gleams in the parquet. Gamblers.
Napes of necks held tight
In gallooned collars.
He moves on. A servant in stockings and white wig
Inclines his shoulders.
The footmen stand in a row, and the tapers

4 Petr Ershov, "Odesskaia literaturnaia kolybel'," *Opyty*, p. 94.
5 Olesha, "Ob Il'fe," in his *Izbrannye sochineniia*, p. 385.
6 Ershov, "Odesskaia literaturnaia kolybel'," p. 95.

Blacken the cupids on the ceiling.
"Hello, Hermann." Leaving the greeting
Unacknowledged, he approaches the table
And with Napoleonic profile
Bends over and stares at the cards . . .]

In Hermann's diseased imagination a vision is formed:

Pochudilas' ulybki prelest'
I plechi v bantakh, vzgliad . . . i vdrug:
Chepets, triasushchaiasia cheliust'
I veny iskudalykh ruk . . .
. . . A posle tiagostno i priamo
Posmotriat mertvye glaza,
I liazhet pikovaia dama
Vzamen schastlivogo tuza! . . .

[He had a fleeting vision of a charming smile,
Beribboned shoulders, a glance . . . and suddenly:
The cap, the trembling jaw
The veins of the emaciated hands . . .
. . . And afterwards the dead eyes
Stare oppressively, straight at him—
And the Queen of Spades turns up
Instead of the lucky Ace.]

A literal translation obscures both the highly successful control of alliteration in the first stanza and a perhaps unfortunate choice of verb. As Aleksei Tolstoi noted on the occasion when he came to hear the young poets read, *Koptiat amurov* may give the impression that the cupids are being cured, like hams.[7] Olesha was considerably deflated by Tolstoi's opinion. Lulled by the praises of his friends and of Odessa critics (one of whom had baptized Olesha's cycle "*Pushkiniany*"), he had saved his own works to read last, as the

[7] Olesha, "Vstrechi s Alekseem Tolstym," *Izbr. soch.*, p. 394.

pièce de résistance. Although Olesha later described these poems as excessively mannered and too much influenced by Igor Severianin,[8] at the time he had though rather well of them.

Soon Olesha and others of the young Odessa writers went to Moscow, where they exchanged the warmth of the poets' collective for the comradeship of a newspaper office. Part of Olesha became "Zubilo," the Chisel, a pseudonym under which he wrote caustic, agitational verse for *Gudok* [*The Whistle*], the railroad workers' paper.

In one of his punning jingles, "Zubilo" explained his function:

Ia ni slova ne pribavil—
Tut ne vymysly moi!
Nikogo ne obesslavil,
Ne podkladyval svin'i.

Razve v tom moia otrada?
Net! Po dolzhnosti moei
Ne podkladyvat' mne nado,
A obkladyvat' svinei.[9]

[I have added not a word—
I haven't made all this up!
I've slandered no one,
And done no one dirt.

Do I really take pleasure in this?
No! In the line of duty
I should bawl no one out unjustly,
But give swine, who deserve it, what for.]

[8] *Ni dnia*, p. 134. According to Aleksandr Spolianskii, a classmate of Olesha throughout his high-school years, Olesha had always displayed a rather high opinion of himself as an adolescent poet—again on the model of Pushkin.

[9] Recorded in Lev Levin, *Na znakomye temy*, p. 108.

Il'f and Petrov, Kataev and Bulgakov worked long hours beside "Zubilo." Olesha enjoyed this work, and did it with the same enthusiasm Maiakovskii brought to *Rosta,* where, in an enormous glacial room, he painted posters which were day-to-day comments on the events of the civil war and the period of foreign intervention.

"Zubilo" was eagerly read; and Kornelii Zelinskii has noted: "His name could move people like a war cry. A railroad station was almost named after him."[10] A peasant who condemned Olesha's novel *Envy* [*Zavist'*] still recalled "Zubilo" enthusiastically: "I often used to read 'Zubilo.' How clever he was! And then he wrote such a bad novel." Another peasant had remembered one of "Zubilo's" punning lines for six years. " 'The old woman's so crabby, her head is like a turnip' [*Baba svirepa, golova kak repa*]. How well he wrote!"[11]

The *Gudok* period held the same privileged position in Olesha's memory as battlefield fellowship often does for others. Olesha rode the open platforms of trains in snow storms and recalled feeling warm inside because engineers and bearded men in sheepskins called him "friend."[12] Banal as this sounds, it was extremely important to Olesha, especially in retrospect. For a brief time he was successfully integrated into a revolutionary collective which embraced but did not stifle him. In the peculiarly enthusiastic atmosphere of the early twenties, "Zubilo" and Olesha the artist were complementary and interdependent, not mutually exclusive. It would seem that Olesha had no need then to use his writing as a weapon to assert his individual existence. For a moment, he realized his ambition

10 Kornelii Zelinskii, "Zmeia v bukete," in *Kriticheskie pis' ma,* p. 129.

11 A. Toporov, *Krest'iane o pisateliakh,* pp. 174, 177. This curious book records the comments of a group of peasants on a number of works of literature. They object strenuously to Olesha's fanciful devices in a "serious" book: "Things move and are alive. There's a live couch there. I didn't like that. It's all lies."

12 *Ni dnia,* p. 142.

to be one with the Revolution and the workers: "Everything was one there, my youth, and the youth of my Soviet Homeland, and the youth of our press, our journalism. . . ."[13]

During the second half of the 1920s, Olesha produced most of his major works: a revolutionary fairytale, ostensibly for children, *The Three Fat Men* [*Tri tolstiaka*]; *Envy* [*Zavist'*], a short novel; and a series of short stories, among them "Liompa," "Love" ["Liubov' "], and "The Cherry Stone" ["Vishnevaia kostochka"]. They are, in the literal sense of the word, brilliant. Rapidly moving, playful, visually inventive, written in a flexible accomplished Russian by a cultivated and highly literate author, *Envy* and the short stories are a joy to read. Some Western critics have gone so far as to say that *Envy* is a great novel, perhaps the greatest novel of the Soviet period.[14]

As Olesha's first published book, *Envy*[15] brought him immediate fame to complement the renown he had won among a different public as "Zubilo." *Envy* was immediately acclaimed for its wit and freshness of description. But after an initial burst of enthusiasm in which even the *Pravda* reviewer participated, Soviet critics who read the text more carefully began to realize that behind the derisive humor and bright colors the vision of the world expressed in *Envy* was a fundamentally

[13] *Ibid.*, p. 140.

[14] See Edward J. Brown, *Russian Literature Since the Revolution*, p. 87; William E. Harkins' comments on the jacket of Andrew R. MacAndrew, ed., Iurii Olesha, *Envy and Other Works.* The recent publication of Bulgakov's *The Master and Margarita* [*Master i Margarita*] should put the much more lightweight and fragile *Envy* back into its true slot as a minor masterpiece.

[15] Iurii Olesha, "Zavist'," *Krasnaia nov'*, No. 7 (1927), pp. 64-101; No. 8 (1927), pp. 3-46. The canonical edition would seem to be the one published (as were many other early Soviet texts) in Berlin in 1931. *Zavist'* (Berlin: "Kniga i stsena," 1931). It was reprinted both in Olesha's *Selected Works* [*Izbrannye sochineniia*] and in his *Tales and Short Stories* [*Povesti i rasskazy*]. As it is the one most widely available, I have chosen to use the 1956 *Izbr. soch.* text. It contains only occasional and insignificant discrepancies from the 1931 text.

solipsistic and selfish one which defied interpretation in a positive socialist sense.[16]

Envy is the story of two cultivated and slightly ridiculous men, Nikolai Kavalerov and Ivan Babichev, whose emotional ties to a bygone time and whose very modes of apprehending the world make them total misfits in the Soviet society which rises around them. They struggle against the builders of Communism (represented by Andrei Babichev, Ivan's brother, who is Director of the Food Trust, and by his protégé, the athletic Volodia Makarov) for possession of the glorious future, incarnate in the person of Ivan's daughter Valia. Kavalerov, who narrates the first part of the novel, is a failure, a hack, who knows he is finished, good only for writing burlesques. Soviet critics soon identified Olesha with Kavalerov. It is important to note, however, that Olesha intended his novel about a man who failed to cope with the Soviet world to be the foundation of his own Soviet fame. At the time, he did not feel tied to the fate of his antihero, but only to the vision with which he had endowed him: "Yes, Kavalerov looked at the world with my eyes. Kavalerov's colors, lighting effects, images, comparisons, metaphors, and conclusions belonged to me. And they were the freshest, brightest colors which I saw."[17]

It shortly became clear, however, that precisely the vision he shared with Kavalerov would make Olesha himself incapable of dealing artistically with the new world in a fashion acceptable to it. By 1929 Olesha was already embroiled in con-

16 By 1931 Soviet criticism was almost unanimous in rejecting the novel on what were essentially political grounds. A study of this reversal of opinion may be found in John Toman's 1958 Columbia University Russian Institute Master's Essay: "Iurii Olesha: Soviet Criticism of his Thought and Literary Expression."

17 Olesha, "Rech' na pervom vsesoiuznom s'ezde sovetskikh pisatelei," in *Povesti i rasskazy*, p. 426. In this study, my ellipses will be indicated by [. . .] to distinguish them from Olesha's frequent use of three dots to indicate a break in thought.

stant and exhausting polemics and self justifications. Such works of the early 1930s as "Something from the Secret Notebooks of Fellow-Traveler Zand" ["Koe-chto iz sekretnykh zapisei poputchika Zanda," 1932], the fragmentary "The Death of Zand" ["Smert' Zanda," 1930], and the play *The List of Blessings* [*Spisok blagodeianii,* 1931], made up a series of transparent self-apologies. In them, Olesha declares that to be an artist is to be afflicted, to be sick. He says that to describe a passion one must have the bacteria of what one describes in oneself. For an artist, this means not so much observing others and their passions as looking for others in oneself. Thus, Olesha's literary preoccupations became increasingly narrow and self-absorbed, almost self-pitying. What new works he did undertake[18] dealt almost exclusively either with the problems of being an artist or with such acts of retaliatory violence as crimes of passion. Young with the century, he now had trouble keeping up with it and felt old and outmoded at thirty. Ironically, Olesha had become like Kavalerov, the character he had created. In his speech to the First Congress of the Soviet Writer's Union, Olesha declared:

> As an artist, I displayed through Kavalerov the purest of strengths, the strength of a first work, of the imparting of first impressions. And then they said that Kavalerov was vulgar and worthless. Because I knew that much of myself was in Kavalerov, I myself felt accused of being worthless and vulgar and was shaken by it. [. . .]
>
> I could not believe that a man who observes attentively and sees the world freshly and in his own way could be vulgar and worth-

[18] Much of Olesha's small production is made up of adaptations of his own previous works. *The Conspiracy of Feelings* [*Zagovor chuvstv*] was a stage version of *Envy.* He turned *The Three Fat Men* into a play for the Moscow Art Theatre. Olesha also adapted the works of other writers. In the 1950s he wrote a dramatization of Dostoevskii's *The Idiot;* and one of his last works was a stage version of Chekhov's "Late-Blooming Flowers" ["Tsvety zapozdalye"].

less. [. . .] I began to think that what I took for a treasure was in fact a sign of poverty. (pp. 426-27)

In the same speech, however, Olesha announced that he had found a new subject which would allow him to keep writing out of the youthful freshness of his sensations. The subject was to be the new Soviet youth. When Olesha's new effort was banned, (*A Strict Youth* [*Strogii iunosha*], a film for which he had written the scenario), a long silence closed over him. It was broken by an occasional story published in Turkestan, where he lived during World War II, by a few newspaper pieces, and by some antifascist film scenarios.[19]

Olesha had, however, continued to write. Fighting a growing difficulty in meeting his own increasingly severe standards, he worked and reworked memories of childhood, impressions, fragments. He kept on writing until his death in 1960, clinging to the practice of his art as to life itself. Only through art could he be seen by others as he wished to be seen. Art gave his life form and meaning; it embraced his life like a sky.

Olesha once wrote: "Man's powerlessness before certain phenomena of nature and life is a subject for transformation by the power of art into splendid images. It is for this that art exists. It is the bridge between man's dream of perfection and the imperfection of his nature."[20] This quotation provides a key to the various aims Olesha set his art and helps to explain why the practice of his art was so vital for him. He considered that art had the moral function of aiding men to recover from

19 Paul Babitsky and John Rimberg, *The Soviet Film Industry*, pp. 151, 179. They list "Val'ter" (1937) ; "Peatbog Soldiers" ["Bolotnye soldaty"] (1938), which deals with a camp in Germany where members of the German Communist Party struggle against Nazi atrocities; and "Engineer Kochin's Error" ["Oshibka inzhenera Kochina"] (1940), which presents an ideal Soviet man who works for the NKVD. Extracts from "Val'ter" were published as "Noch'," in *30 dnei*, No. 4 (1937), pp. 15-23.

20 Olesha, "Iurii Olesha Talks with His Readers," trans. H. O. Whyte, *International Literature*, No. 3 (1936), p. 88.

alienation. He demanded that Communism develop as a moral system, a human system, not merely as an economic system,[21] and was convinced that it was the artist's role to be the guardian of the humanist ethic which envisages the Communist future as the time of the achievement of man's wholeness: "I want to depict man for the first time becoming *Man*, freed from the domination of money. [. . .] humanity's worth—intelligence, inventiveness, aspiration towards perfection, thirst for knowledge, poetry, nobility of character."[22]

Although there is no evidence that Olesha had studied Marx carefully, the above declaration resembles Marx's and Engels' formula for the whole man:

> Man adopts his all-sided being in an all-sided manner, in other words as a total man. Every one of his human relations with the world: seeing, hearing, smelling, tasting, feeling, thinking, contemplating, willing, acting, loving, in short all the organs of his individuality as well as organs which in their immediate form are common to all [. . .][23]

Literature could aid in the creation of fully conscious and perceptive individualities:

21 "Rech'," pp. 429-30.

22 Olesha, "Literatura—obshchee delo pisatelia i rabochego," *Literaturnaia gazeta*, December 17, 1933.

23 Karl Marx and Friedrich Engels, *Literature and Art: Selections from Their Writings*, p. 61. Olesha does quote Marx occasionally, e.g., "Strogii iunosha" in *Izbrannoe*, p. 243. It is tantalizing to note that Marx and Engels characterized the new bourgeoisie as "sausage makers." Andrei Babichev, the interim man in *Envy*, is a sausage maker. All of *Envy*, moreover, might be treated under the aegis of their comment: "If the decline of former classes—such as the knight, for instance—could furnish material for magnificent works of art, the *petite bourgeoisie* naturally provides nothing but feeble manifestations of fanatical malice, nothing but collections of phrases and sayings in the manner of Sancho Panza." (From the French selection of Marx's and Engels' writings, *Sur la littérature et l'art*, ed. Jean Fréville, pp. 18-19.)

It would be worth while creating hundreds of literary miracles [such as a favorite scene from Tolstoi]. What for? To show people how other men have been able to think and see. Why show them this? So that those who are unable to think and see like that still esteem themselves at that moment, understanding that because they too are human, they too are capable of much. (*Ni dnia*, p. 206)

For Olesha, art could also have another liberating function. It could temporarily overcome man's helplessness before his animal and human situation by creating within the work of art a world where the limitations to which human existence is normally subject seem to be abolished. In Olesha's works, the laws of gravity and normal vision seem broken. The reader is removed from the adult, rational world where effect follows cause and result follows effort. He has returned to a stage of perception where magical changes and transformations seem to occur. The system of the world seems to have been destroyed.

The important word here, however, is *seems.* Olesha does not write the kind of fantasy where inexplicable things are asserted to have really happened. He makes it clear that the shattering of the normal structures of the world is a function of the perceiving sensibility within the work. The perceiver is the center of a system, the stable element, altering everything around him by his idiosyncratic apprehension of it, but altering it in this way only. Thus, the perceiver compensates for his feeling of lack of control over the world in which he exists.

In almost all his nonpolemical works, Olesha presents to his reader the spectacle of imagined triumphs over the world. Not only do the heroes of his stories exercise such control, but Olesha also writes many small sketches wherein he makes no effort to create a fictional character, but simply exercises, without intermediary, his own power to control the world by an idiosyncratic perception of it.

Thus, the major effort of Olesha's art is to achieve the illusion of control. And, double blessing, as an artist Olesha has the hope that the activity which enables him to appropriate a distorted world will bring him fame in the real world and make him a master of life as well. Indeed, beyond the splendid liberating images of the book itself, in which every reader may share, the artist obtains still another benefit from his work. Olesha the artist watches his character looking at things in order that the artist himself may be seen by others. The ultimate motivation of Olesha's writing is to make a place for himself in his society and to control the image others have of him.

He had a desperate longing for fame. Vladimir Lidin records that when western Belo-Russia returned to Russian sovereignty in 1939 Olesha refused to take this long-awaited opportunity to go and see his parents, who were then living in Grodno. Olesha is said to have declared: "Not now, I'll go home when I'm famous and have lots of money, so that the whole town will say, 'The Oleshas' son has come.' " Lidin, a close friend of Olesha's at the time, is sure that Olesha was actually convinced that only such a triumphant return could really make his parents happy[24]—and make Olesha happy.

Olesha's works are permeated by the yearnings for glory of both his ostensibly fictional heroes and of his admittedly autobiographical ones. He was not content to be remembered simply as the author of certain works of fiction. It was not enough that he considered *Envy* to be immortal.[25] He wanted a personal, legendary renown like Maiakovskii's, and as he aged he became more and more concerned with preserving his living personality, consciously attempting to fix his life as an artist, to achieve the transformation of his perishable existence into a work of which he is not only the author, but also the avowed,

24 Vladimir Lidin, *Liudi i vstrechi*, pp. 116-17.
25 *Ni dnia*, p. 161.

literal subject. For as he once declared to Lidin, "The artist is a pearl in the maw of time."[26]

It is no accident that Olesha speaks of the artist, not the work, as a pearl: a rare, precious object, formed by chance in a destructive world. For him, the work is primarily the means by which the artist can define and preserve his own image of his talent so that others may see it. This book is an attempt to analyse the means Olesha employs in his effort to make himself visible to the world. It will trace his search for self-definition, domination, and control as this quest appears in the images, themes, and devices characteristic of Olesha's vivid, yet peculiarly cautious, artistic imagination.

Much previous criticism of Olesha has focused on *Envy* and a few early short stories.[27] Admittedly, these are Olesha's best works, the ones which refract the most light, the ones he wrote with the greatest ease. The widely held picture of Olesha as a basically joyous, comic writer destroyed by Soviet conditions is a result of this concentration of attention. So is the speculation that Olesha might, otherwise and elsewhere, have continued to develop into "a great writer."

Consideration of a broader range of Olesha's writing reveals a more interesting, if less endearing, imagination. He is an artist in a much more complex relation to Soviet reality than may appear the case when one concentrates on a small number of the best early works.

In an effort to redress the balance, I shall insist, perhaps somewhat heavily, on the more somber, grotesque aspects of Olesha's imagination, and devote proportionally less attention to *Envy* than might be expected. Similarly, the analysis of in-

26 Lidin, p. 119.

27 One important exception is Gleb Struve's study in his *Soviet Russian Literature 1917-50.* A. Bilenkov's forthcoming book should also help provide a more balanced estimate of the significance of Olesha's whole career.

dividual works does not intend to be exhaustive,[28] but rather to reveal, even in the seemingly carefree early works like "Love," the lineaments of an almost never satisfied desire for freedom, domination, and control.

[28] This is particularly true of the analysis of *Envy*. I shall deal with the complexities of its construction in a book on narrative structure in the novels of the 1920s.

Chapter I

Art as a Means of Knowing and Possessing the World

Many of Olesha's works are concerned with the relationship of imaginative artistic creation to other human activities, and with the practice of art as a mode of dealing with the world. We can therefore approach these problems directly through an analysis of Olesha's story "The Cherry Stone,"[1] which is about an artist's effort to assert the interdependence of art and life.

On its simplest level, "The Cherry Stone" may be read as the story of a writer who tries to integrate the work of his imagination into the Five-Year Plan. There are two spheres of action in the story: the "invisible land" and Soviet reality. The invisible land is the world of artistic synthesis. The writer hero, Fedia, walks there hand in hand with two sisters, Observation [*Vnimanie*] and Imagination [*Voobrazhenie*], uniting them in his person. This is a formula for the writer's creative task. In the invisible land of artistic imagination, the hero can cause a cherry tree to spring from a pit he has appropriated from the real world. If he wishes to actualize his private vision and make it accessible to everyone, he must bring it forth from the invisible land into the world. The artist therefore makes a book.[2] This action is symbolized by Fedia's setting the pit in the soil of a vacant lot.

1 Olesha, "Vishnevaia kostochka," *Izbr. soch.*, pp. 261-69.

2 There is a clear metaphorical link betwen the book and the tree. Fedia even describes its blossoming as "this paper tree." [*Eto bumazhnoe derevo*].

Abel, a literal-minded worker (marked by his very name as the Righteous One whose offerings are pleasing to Authority), brings a delegation of visitors to the site of the buried pit. He asks them to use their imaginations to visualize not a cherry tree but the enormous building that is to rise on the lot. The hero realizes that his tree is not only unnecessary to the world of the Plan but doomed to destruction by it:

> . . . Dear Natasha, I forgot the most important thing—the Plan. There is a Plan. I acted without consulting the Plan. In five years a concrete giant will be erected on this site where now there is nothing but emptiness, a ditch, and useless walls. My sister, Imagination, is a hasty person. In the spring, they will begin to lay the foundation—and then where will my silly cherry pit be! Yet, there in the invisible land, the tree I dedicated to you will someday bloom. . . .
>
> Tourists will come to see the concrete giant.
>
> They won't see your tree. Is it really impossible to make an invisible land visible? . . . (p. 269)

But a miraculous reconciliation takes place:

> "The building will be laid out in a semi-circle," said Abel. "The whole interior of the semi-circle will be filled by a garden. Have you an imagination?"
>
> "Yes," I said. "I see it, Abel. I see it clearly. Here there will be a garden, and there, on the spot where you're standing, a cherry tree will grow." (p. 269)

Thus, the tree conceived in the invisible land becomes visible, a pleasure to all. It is important to note, however, that Olesha makes a clear distinction between the world of art and the world of the Plan. The work of art appears as an element of play and relaxation alongside the functional, concrete construction of the Plan. Art may beautify the world of the Plan and complement it, but the vision of the artist is of a different nature from that of a builder.

Nevertheless, both visions are actualized and together form a harmony. By asserting the existence of such a complementary relationship, Olesha can feel that his realization is no less manly than that of a builder. Olesha was very touchy about this, and felt obliged to state publicly:

> Sometimes I think that to be a poet, an artist, is to be a weak man. It's a childish profession. I think about the fact that in the world there are men and children. And the men build and struggle. The children sing.
>
> Sometimes I want to be a builder, a warrior. But suddenly I realize that many of those whom I consider men—warriors, builders—dream of writing. Thus a harmony is established. And I can be a writer once more. They say that even Napoleon wrote a novel.[3]

Olesha makes a point of the fact that great men have wanted to be writers because he is aware that, particularly in the Soviet Union of the first Five-Year Plan, imaginative creative activity might be considered primarily a compensation for failure in other domains. Indeed, the second level of treatment in "The Cherry Stone" of art's relation to the world is directed precisely to this problem. Fedia avows the fact that he plants his tree, creates his work of art, to compensate for his failure to be loved:

> I planted a tree in memory of the fact that you didn't love me. [. . .] I was ridiculous then; Boris Mikhailovich was the manly one who conquered you. I was dreamy, infantile. I was looking for a thrush in the world while you were kissing. I was a romantic. But look: a hard, manly tree has grown from the seed of the romantic. [. . .] Believe me, Natasha, romanticism is a manly thing, and one shouldn't deride it. . . . (p. 266)

[3] Olesha, quoted in an interview by Vl. Sobolev, "Guliaia v sadu, "*Literaturnaia gazeta,* May 29, 1933.

It is not by chance that Olesha made a cherry tree the symbol of Fedia's artistic creativity. However much Fedia denies his childishness and declares that romanticism is a manly thing, he nonetheless chooses to imagine his tree in its time of blossom, of innocent beauty. Olesha deliberately opposes the image of the flowering tree to that of its fruit. In general, he associates fruit with consummated love, and flowers with a more abstract, dreamy attachment. He connects the juiciness of fruit with physical attraction, and its color and roundness with a physical fulfillment or well-being which is usually, but not always, sexual.[4]

Therefore, Fedia the dreamer and his rival Boris Mikhailovich react quite differently to the invitation of ripe cherries. Both young men are in the woods with Natasha. Stained with dark juice, she offers cherries to them both. Fedia keeps a pit in his mouth in "childish habit," while Boris Mikhailovich kisses the waiting Natasha. Fedia, however, makes it clear that a work of art can more than make up for such a failure in life.

If Boris Mikhailovich had caught me squatting in the vacant lot, planting my infantile cherry pit, he would once more have sensed his victory over me. The victory of a man over a dreamer. But during that time, I planted a seed in the earth. It split and brought forth a blinding explosion. I sowed my seed in the earth. This tree is my child by you, Natasha. Bring your son, begotten by Boris

[4] Fruits appear very often in Olesha's works as the basis of images of blessedness. Even in *Ni dnia bez strochki*, they are still among his favorite subjects for metaphor-making (pp. 258, 183). In "Liubov'," the hero's mistress is seen eating apricots. In *Zavist'*, Kavalerov, in a moment of rather ambivalent sexual jealousy, sees that Volodia's sock "had slipped down and formed a green doughnut around a pearlike calf, lightly covered with hair" (*Izbr. soch.*, p. 121). On the one occasion when Kavalerov sees Valia as a solid, earthy being, rather than as an aerial, flowery one, he compares her knees with oranges (p. 113). Kavalerov sees himself as a fruit too, but as a soft, overripe one, good for nothing, falling helplessly to the ground (p. 69).

Mikhailovich. I will look and see whether he is as healthy, pure, and absolute as this tree which was begotten by an infantile fellow.[5] (p. 266)

Dreamers, says Fedia, should not produce children, but "trees for the new world." (p. 267)

The substitution of trees for children and works of art for success in love is in some sense a public sublimation. But Olesha's hero also has several other private compensations which remain within the boundaries of his personal invisible land. Natasha has made a date to meet him at a tram stop. He waits, and she doesn't come. People ask him for directions, and he jumps at the opportunity to change his situation in the eyes of others:

No one must know that I'm waiting for my date. Better let them think: "The broadly smiling young man has come out to the street-corner in order to help people; he will tell us everything, direct us, calm us. . . . Let's go to him!" [. . .] Let's forget about the date. I'm not in love. I'm the good genie of the street. Come to me! Come to me! (p. 263)

Fedia imagines himself in a position superior to people who are lost or uncertain precisely in order to escape from his own uncertainty. He is in a typical situation for an Olesha character.[6] Everyone else goes on about his business. Only he waits, with nothing in the world to do:

[5] Olesha also gives the name Boris Mikhailovich to his hero's successful rival in the unfinished play about a theatre doctor on which he was working around 1934.

[6] Olesha himself seems to have spent an appreciable amount of time on street corners, where, as often as not, he too served as guide and information booth. The last section of *Ni dnia bez strochki,* which speaks about the corner-standing of his later years, is called "The Amazing Crossroad" ["Udivitel'nyi perekrestok"].

The woman has already ridden off in the Number 16 bus, the Red Army man is already wandering through the cool halls of the museum, the chauffeur is already honking his horn on Varsonof'-evskii Avenue. The blind man is already climbing, touchily and self-lovingly, onto the front platform of the bus, his cane before him.

They are all satisfied, all happy.

But I keep on standing, smiling idiotically. (p. 264)

To escape from a real position of total powerlessness, Fedia retreats into the invisible land of his imagination where he revenges himself by becoming a policeman, a figure of authority: "Oh, look, there's a whistle between my lips. . . . I whistle. . . . I have the right to whistle. . . . Children, envy me! [. . .] Congratulate me, Natasha, I've turned into a policeman. . . ." (p. 265)

Fedia is perplexed by this particular metamorphosis (although, to the reader, it is clearly in response to a situation he cannot control) because it does not correspond to the conception Fedia has of the unlimited nature of his power in the invisible land:

And do you know the most surprising thing about it, Abel? It's that for some reason or other I play the part of a policeman in this enchanting land. . . . I would have thought that I should travel through the invisible land calmly and majestically, and the flowering staff of a prophet should gleam in my hand. . . . (p. 265)

For him, his invisible land is the sphere of his effortless, almost magic control. It is the land where he is fully master, which he calls a "third world." When he walks with Observation and Imagination in this land: [. . .] "in spite of everything, in spite of the established order and society, don't I create a world which is subject to no laws except the illusory laws of my own sensations?" (p. 263)[7]

Observation tends to be subordinated to imagination in this process. The artist's commitment to transformation by imagination may prevent him from observing accurately in the first place. Let us consider, for example, how Fedia sees the ant hills.

The last time I saw an ant hill was about twenty years ago. Oh, of course, I've happened to walk on ant hills, probably many times in the course of those twenty years. And I probably saw them, but, having noticed them, I didn't think "I'm treading on ant hills." The words "ant hill" simply outlined themselves in my consciousness, and that was all. The live image was instantly shoved out by the term which obediently came to hand. (p. 267)

This time Fedia decides to look closely at the ant hills. But even now, he chooses to look from a vantage point which precludes factual knowledge and produces an agreeable illusion:

From my full height I couldn't see the ants. My vision caught only a certain disturbance of forms which one could just as well consider motionless, and my vision willingly yielded to the illusion. I looked and was willing to think that these weren't a multitude of ants swarming around the ant hills, but the ant hills themselves, crumbling like dunes. (p. 268)

Similarly, because of his fascination with the ant hills, Fedia throws away a stone he had picked up. Too late, he hears the

[7] Although he is no Symbolist, Fedia's musings on the "third world" created by the artistic imagination of the writer echo Andrei Belyi: "The word creates a new, third world—a world of sound symbols, by means of which the secrets of the world which exists beyond myself as well as the secrets which are locked within me are illuminated. [. . .] Through sound, a new world is recreated, within whose borders I feel myself the creator of reality. Then, I begin to name objects. That is, I resurrect them a second time for myself." ("Magiia slov," *Simvolizm*, p. 430).

voice of the stone, asking to be looked at. He cannot find it again. But the stone itself is no great loss. Not bound by any knowledge of it, Fedia can imagine the stone as being perhaps a compound, or a stone with a fossil imbedded in it, perhaps not a stone at all, but a petrified bone. Imagination can make of the stone what she wills, because Fedia has sacrificed Observation to her. Fedia's vision of the world is therefore in no way scientific, but exclusively poetic. As Albert Béguin puts it: "[. . .] poétique, c'est-à-dire dirigée de l'intérieur vers l'extérieur, percevant le monde par une création, une imagination libre."[8]

Thus, "The Cherry Stone" not only touches on the relation of art to the Five-Year Plan and the problem of artistic activity as a compensation for failure, but also raises the problem of the nature of the artist's vision. The artist does pay attention to the external world. He does look at the physical ant hills instead of merely being satisfied to allow the stale words "ant hill" to block out a live image. And by choosing to observe from an unusual vantage point—in this case, from such a distance that he cannot see the proper relationship of the ants to the hills—he may obtain a "fresh vision" of the object. Olesha tries to provide precisely this kind of "fresh vision" of the physical world in his works.

Of course, many others writers have used similar techniques, and Viktor Shklovskii is talking about just such a way of seeing when he speaks of *ostranenie*, "making strange," a technique of narration whereby a character sees as if for the first time, and thus does not understand the significance of what he sees.[9] To use Professor Leon Stilman's apt formulation, it is perception without apperception. Lev Tolstoi, for instance, uses

[8] Albert Béguin, *L'Ame romantique et le rêve*, p. 97.

[9] Polonskii even uses the term *ostranenie* to describe Olesha's technique. "Ocherki sovremennoi literatury (preodolenie *Zavisti*)," *Novyi mir*, No. 5 (May, 1929), p. 191.

the technique quite often. He records the battle of Sebastopol from a great distance, and in *War and Peace* the battle of Borodino is seen through the eyes of Pierre.

Pierre at first perceives the battle aesthetically. His position is privileged both because he is out of the struggle and because the distance miniaturizes and purifies. He sees the white puffs of cannon smoke out of context, without really understanding their significance. They are a beautiful spectacle, as yet unrelated in Pierre's mind to carnage.[10] The reader, however, knows the true relation of pretty balls of smoke to death, and he watches Pierre learn. Pierre comes to understand the meaning of the glitter and movement when he is surrounded by dead bodies. With the prolonged, piercing cries of a wounded horse in his ears, the smooth balls of smoke which dispersed so prettily become terrible to Pierre.

Tolstoi's purpose in "making strange" differs significantly from Olesha's. Tolstoi uses the device from time to time as a sharp contrast. In Olesha's works it is the usual manner of seeing. Furthermore, as is evident in the passage about Pierre's baptism of fire, Tolstoi intends the reader to *see through* the device, to make some kind of judgment on the basis of the "innocent" vision with which he has been presented. The device has a broader moral purpose. Olesha himself contrasted his own technique with Tolstoi's, saying: "It seems to me that I am only a namer of things. Not even an artist, but just some sort of pharmacist, a wrapper of powders, a pill roller. Tolstoi, who was occupied with moral, or historical, or economic arguments, cast his colors unerringly as he went along. I direct all

10 The texture of Pierre's first vision of the battle is very much like Olesha's in *The Three Fat Men*. The beautiful puffs Pierre sees expanding resemble Olesha's puffs which explode like cotton batting. (*Izbr. soch.*, p. 135). For a detailed discussion of Tolstoi's scene, see Leon Stilman's article "Nabliudeniia nad nekotorymi osobennostiami kompozitsii i stilia v romane Tolstogo *Voina i mir*," in *American Contributions to the Fifth International Congress of Slavists, Sofia, 1963*, pp. 327-35.

my attention to color" (*Ni dnia*, p. 257). It is clear in context that Olesha is not totally serious when he says he is not even an artist, but he has noted an important difference between two different kinds of artistry.

Olesha is primarily interested in giving his works a lively surface, and so he sees as if through an innocent eye all the time, presenting a vision of a world which is "freshly" seen, but many of whose relations are thereby falsified. What kind of knowledge of the world is provided by this kind of art?[11] To what extent does such privileged vision put one in closer relation to the objects of the world around, and to what extent does it, on the contrary, impede one's full possession of the world? Olesha investigates these problems in one of his finest stories, "Liompa."

"Liompa" deals with various ways to relate to the world and possess it: by naming and language, by observing with an innocent eye, and by actually manipulating things. These various modes of encountering one's surroundings are practiced respectively by the dying protagonist Ponomarev, by a very small boy, who comes to visit him, and by an older boy who builds model airplanes.

The critic Lev Levin has stated: "Olesha writes not about reality itself but about various relations to it. [. . .] It is to the

[11] In so far as Olesha was a "formalist" in the beginning of his career, he would have subscribed to Shklovskii's statement: "The purpose of an image is not to make clearer and more comprehensible the signification that it carries, but to create a particular perception of the object, to create its *vision* and not its *recognition*" ("Iskusstvo kak priem," *O teorii prozy*, Moscow, 1929, p. 18). This does not, however, mean that behind his commitment to art as device Olesha was not using this device *for* something: an assertion of idiosyncratic control through the primacy of vision over recognition. Further, while Shklovskii stated that art develops a variety of techniques to *impede* comprehension and automatic perception, to slow the process down, he never proposed that this kind of perception be developed into a *way of life* for a character in a novel, and certainly not for the novel's author.

inner psychological world that Olesha devotes his attention. The outer world has no independent value."[12]

It is true that Olesha writes about relations to reality, but he also writes in "Liompa" about a reality which exists independently of any character's consciousness of it. In fact, the great lesson learned by Ponomarev as he dies is that the world is not a function of his brain. He is not the ruler of things; they do not depend on his knowledge of their names:

"I thought the external world didn't exist," he mused. "I thought that my eyes and ears ruled things; I thought the world would cease to exist when I ceased to exist [. . .] I thought that my brain gave things shape, weight, and color, but they have gone away from me, and their names only, useless names which have lost their masters, swarm in my brain." (p. 273)

Things continue in all their materiality after the eclipse of Ponomarev's consciousness: "Later in the day, a light blue coffin with yellow ornaments appeared in the kitchen. [. . .] The coffin had to be twisted and turned for a long time in order to get it through the door. They banged a shelf, a pot. Plaster fell. The boy, Aleksandr, climbed on the stove and helped, holding the coffin up from below." (p. 274)

Ponomarev's dying is measured by his increasing isolation from things. As N. Berkovskii notes, the process of dying is represented by Olesha as a lessening of mastery over the universe.[13] Dying is a continuous process. Ponomarev has lost control over certain things not because he is ill, but simply because he is aging. Ponomarev feels that death is destroying things on its way to him, leaving him with names only. But

[12] Levin, *Na znakomye temy*, pp. 99, 101.

[13] N. Berkovskii, "O prozaikakh," *Zvezda*, No. 12 (1929), p. 153. Berkovskii concludes: "Only from the point of view of the idealistic appropriation of the universe can such a conception of death arise."

Olesha shows us that the things really remain; that they are not destroyed. On the contrary, it is loss of contact with things which is death. The more Ponomarev is concerned with the names of things, rather than the things themselves, the closer he is to death. Delirious, he searches for the proper name of a rat he thinks he hears in the kitchen.[14] He knows that as soon as he finds the meaningless name he will die. He yells: "Liompa!"—the non-name of a perhaps nonexistent rat.[15] This final dissociation and alienation from reality is the moment of spiritual death, the culmination of the process of aging: the loss of both physical and mental control.

This decline is an inevitable descent from the grace of childhood. A very small boy comes to visit Ponomarev, and despite Ponomarev's effort to keep things with him, they clearly prefer the child: "The little boy walked around. Things rushed to meet him. He smiled at them, not knowing any of their names. He left the room and the magnificent train of things raced after him." (p. 273) This "rubber boy," as Olesha calls him, sees

[14] Ponomarev's struggle with the rat's name is a variation in reverse on Tolstoi's treatment of the dying Prince André's attempt to *identify* things in terms of rational language and thus to hold back death (*Voina i mir*, Book III, Chapter XXXII). Olesha was much given to this kind of literary variation, particularly on themes of Tolstoi and Pushkin. Olesha himself has now become the object of similar compliments by younger writers, e.g., one of the closing scenes of Vasilii Aksenov's *Pora, moi drug, pora*, a novel whose title itself is a quote from Pushkin, pp. 250-51. Aksenov's scene is a variant of the passages in Olesha, particularly in "Koe-chto iz sekretnykh zapisei poputchika Zanda" and *Zavist'*, where pieces of furniture with mirrors on them are carried through the streets.

[15] Olesha leaves it unclear whether or not the rat exists. Ponomarev hears it "cleaning up, rattling the plates, opening the tap, making scraping sounds in the bucket," and then says, "Aha, she's washing the dishes." The feminine pronoun could refer either to a rat, [*krysa*], a feminine noun in Russian, or to a woman. Andrew MacAndrew, in his deft and lively translation published in the collection *The Wayward Comrade and the Commissars*, and reprinted in *Envy and Other Works*, resolves Olesha's deliberate ambiguity by making Ponomarev say "Why someone must be washing dishes in there." (p. 135) The Russian text says simply, "*Ege, ona sudomoika.*"

the world through genuinely innocent eyes. He has no name himself, and no concept of time or change. He has just learned to recognize things, but doesn't yet really deal with them because he has no understanding of relations, particularly causal relations. He cannot hold onto a beam of light. He thinks a bicycle is held to the wall by the scratch its pedal has made. "Lines took shape and joined around him, and bodies formed. Suddenly a wonderful pattern of light would form. The boy would start to rush towards it, but when he had barely taken a step, the change of distance always destroyed the illusion. [. . .] Each second created a new thing for him." (p. 272) But each second also takes away something else. The rubber boy lives in the instant. Playing with light, he is privileged because he has not yet really begun the journey to death, to the other pole, where he will know names but no longer know things. He takes the first step on this road at the end of the story. "When the coffin finally got into the corridor, it immediately became black, and the rubber boy ran in front of it, his sandals slapping on the floor. 'Grandpa! Grandpa!' he shouted, 'They've brought you a coffin.' " (p. 274) He has learned the name of the unwieldly object, although obviously he does not yet understand what it is for.

The next stage of knowledge is that of an older boy named Aleksandr. He is the one person in the story who has a working relationship with things, and who has a definite place in the spatial, temporal, and natural order, in the hierarchy of the universe. "The boy was surrounded by rubber bands, wire, strips of wood, silk—a light, tea rose colored piece of silk—and the smell of glue. The sky glittered. Insects crawled over a stone. The stone had a little petrified shell embedded in it." (p. 272) He is surrounded by things which he uses, and he is making something: a model plane which actually flies. Ponomarev's last futile gesture is an attempt to seize this plane.

Aleksandr has power over things.[16] It is Alexsandr who gets the coffin through the corridor. In general:

[. . .] the boy acted in a completely grown-up way, a way, in fact, in which very few adults are capable of acting: he proceeded completely scientifically. He was using a blueprint in constructing his model, he made calculations and respected the laws of nature. He could have defended himself against the adults' attacks by explaining the laws, demonstrating his experiments, but he kept silent because he did not feel that he had the right to show himself more serious than the adults. (p. 272)

The implication would seem to be that Aleksandr too, as he must become an adult, will lose his full-blooded, direct relationship to things on his way to death.

Before he sinks into delirium, Ponomarev really admits that Aleksandr's mode of relating to the world is the best of the three, because it brings mastery of the physical world, Alexsandr can hold things. Ponomarev and the rubber boy cannot. In "Liompa," the physical world is symbolized by an apple. The apple is a true object of desire, it has—a sign of grace—the power to hold and concentrate light:

There was an apple in the world. It was gleaming amidst the leaves, gently turning, and catching and turning with itself bits of the day, the azure of the garden, the window frame. The law of gravity was waiting for it under the tree. [. . .] There were many causes hidden in the apple, causes that could determine a multitude of effects, but none of these causes were intended for Ponomarev. The apple had become an abstraction to him. And the fact that the flesh of the thing had disappeared for him while only the abstraction remained was a torment. (pp. 272-73)

16 Olesha himself could never make model planes. He writes that he could not even put together cardboard cutouts. He was too impatient with the pretraced lines, and wanted only "free creativity." (*Ni dnia*, p. 36).

Yet, Ponomarev does not envy Aleksandr, who both controls the flesh of things and is aware of the abstractions which govern them. Ponomarev envies instead the rubber boy, who perceives only the flesh, the "thingness" of an object, but does not know what it is for. Ponomarev is nostalgic for an innocent vision which does not understand relations, and does not entail a responsible attitude to the things which surround him.

On the one hand, there is the boy's primitive perception without names—a state of prelanguage bliss. On the other hand, Ponomarev represents a knowledge of the world which exists only in terms of words. He possesses it only by knowing the names of things. At the very end, however, Ponomarev loses contact even with the communicative function of language. His naming of the rat "Liompa" marks the final destruction of semantic structures. When you call a thing by a name which does not belong to it, loss of contact with the world is complete, and this is death—or poetry.

Olesha's recognition in "Liompa" of the possibility of a final dissociation between the namer and what he names reflects his uneasiness as to the nature of poetic language, which also rejects the merely practical, communicative function of language. He shared the rather common anguish of writers who realize that those who occupy themselves in a struggle to bend language to their wills are increasingly cut off from things. Thus, paradoxically, mastery of poetic language may estrange the writer more and more from the physical world with which, in Olesha's case, the practice of art was intended to cope. Olesha recognizes that if by his art he compensates for a dominance he cannot have over reality, his use of art in this way threatens to alienate him still further from "the brilliant carnival" of the rising new world, from the apple, from the things which remain his heart's desire.

Olesha's awareness that poetic language is a sacrilege against practical language is particularly acute because his primary use for it is to attempt to recreate the rubber boy's perception of the world and to transmit this fresh, nonfunctional vision. Of course, Olesha cannot really create through language a perception defined as being prelinguistic. He can only approximate it through metaphor and simile: the naming of things by names which are not their own. Metaphor and simile have little in common with the processes of childish vision itself, but they do provide the adult reader with an impression of freshness.

Although simile and metaphor are basic components of almost any poetic language, they are exceptionally important to Olesha's. He is aware that his own gift consists primarily in his ability to name things by other names, so much so that when in his later years he wonders whether he can still write, he couches his doubts in terms of whether or not he can still give birth to metaphors.[17]

Olesha's use of terms to designate simile and metaphor is confused and misleading. He applies the word "metaphor" indiscriminately to both metaphor and simile. In *No Day without a Line*, for example, Olesha writes a little parable of his artistic career, describing how he had opened a Metaphor Shop.[18] He had a lovely stock of metaphors, but people would buy only the run-of-the-mill ones like "pale as death." What interests us here is that "pale as death" is not a metaphor at all. It is a simile, a comparison, rather than an imaginative fusion of two elements. Olesha goes on to express his disappointment that no one wanted one of his favorite items: "It was a metaphor about a pool under a tree on an autumn day. It said that the pool lay under the tree like a gypsy woman." (p. 268) This "metaphor" is a simile too. Olesha therefore

[17] *Ni dnia,* p. 255.
[18] *Ibid.,* pp. 257-58.

obscures the fact that he usually makes simple comparisons, talking of them as though they had the more durable imaginative reality of metaphor.

Olesha's attitude toward his "metaphors" is ambivalent. Often he declares that he considers them only tools, devices to make everyone a poet, to return to every reader a fresher perception of the world: "[. . .] the point of a metaphor is that the artist prompts the reader to define a resemblance which already crossed the reader's mind but which he had never formulated."[19] In "Iurii Olesha Talks with his Readers," he rejects what he calls "winks" on the part of the author. Metaphors, comparisons, and decorative epithets

> [. . .] must not, in any circumstances, dare to be "remarks" on the part of the author. They must not stick out of the fabric of narration. When, on coming across a metaphor or some kind of definition, you see the winking of the eye of the author through the web of narration—it is disgusting. "There," he seems to say, "what a nice thing I've thought up." [. . .] Such private comparisons should not be made. Everything is like everything else. (p. 85)

Metaphors, definitions, and coloration should not be allowed to dominate the narrative structure. Olesha upbraids Bunin on these very grounds and condemns him for loading down his "The Gentleman from San Francisco" ["Gospodin iz San Francisco"] with unnecessary similes, details, and colors. Olesha concludes: "Finally a story is not the proliferation of a series of colors and epithets. [. . .] In the end, we writers know that everything resembles everything else, and the power of prose is not in colors." (*Ni dnia,* p. 245)

His harsh condemnation of Bunin sounds curiously like the reproaches made by critics against *Envy.* For Olesha goes on to declare:

[19] Olesha, "Literaturnaia tekhnika," *Izbr. soch.*, p. 427.

Bunin has no faith, only nostalgia for his past youth, occasioned by the dying out of sensibility. . . .

His musings about the soul's merging with infinity and suchlike, seem sometimes merely stupid. The notorious "Gentleman from San Francisco" is utterly gloomy; colors are piled one on another until one is nauseated. A criticism of the bourgeois world? I don't think so. Bunin's own fear of death, his envy of the young and the rich, even a sort of servility. (p. 246)

Olesha's hatred of Bunin[20] seems to some degree self-hatred. For Olesha himself had once affirmed that if he had it to do over again he would write *Envy* differently and curb the over-abundance of color and imagery.[21] On the other hand, he considers *Envy* as it stands to be "immortal,"[22] and immortal precisely because of all the "metaphors" in it. Despite the fact that he sometimes states that metaphoric language is only a tool, his deepest conviction is that "metaphor" is what is eternal in art.[23] In fact, with Olesha the priorities often become reversed: the work of art becomes primarily a pretext for making striking comparisons.

Olesha enjoyed improvising such "metaphors," and mentally collected those made by others which struck his fancy. His attitude toward Khlebnikov's animal imagery, for example, is particularly revealing. He is interested only in the metaphors themselves, not in Khlebnikov's purpose in formulating them.[24] Olesha himself was interested in animals as raw material for comparisons. His sketch about a trip to the zoo, "We Are in

20 One must not discount Olesha's strong personal dislike for Bunin. He records his first accidental meeting with Bunin in such a way as to indicate dislike even before he found out who he was. (*Ni dnia*, p. 122) Viktor Vinogradov accuses Olesha of unwillingness and perhaps even a narrow-minded inability to penetrate Bunin's poetic system and style. (*Stilistika, Teoriia poeticheskoi rechi, Poetika*, p. 191.)

21 "Talks with his Readers," p. 84.

22 *Ni dnia*, p. 161.

23 *Ibid.*, p. 257.

24 *Ibid.*, pp. 259-60.

the Center of Town" ["My v tsentre goroda"], is a preparatory exercise for comparison-making. Olesha observes the animals carefully, describes them affectionately, and then tries to see what *else* they look like. The kangaroo, for example, reminds him of a dog. He praises Walt Disney because Disney has realized how much animals are like people, and the fact that one can both describe people in terms of the animals they most resemble and describe animals in terms of human beings.[25] Olesha himself works in both directions, but he particularly likes to use an animal as the tenor of a simile and then ring a series of comparisons on it. He declares: "Oh, I can draw from any muzzle, even the smallest, a whole string of comparisons (similes). The source of artistry never runs dry when you are looking at a wild animal."[26]

One cannot help observing, however, that many of Olesha's "metaphors" are like the animals he sees in the zoo—isolated from their native habitat, presented caged for the distraction of the spectator. Olesha himself would seem to recognize this when he says, comparing himself to Kataev: "Kataev writes better than I. He has written a great deal. I have written only fragments. A collection of metaphors."[27]

Olesha's attitude toward metaphors and similes is basically a playful one. He does not limit them, as Kataev tends to do, to a strictly expressive and utilitarian function. Olesha's view of his basic devices therefore has important implications for the kind of knowledge of the world which his works provide.

In the first place, there are many comparisons on a typical page of Olesha's fiction. As these comparisons are usually made through the use of simile rather than metaphor, the objects

25 Olesha, "My v tsentre goroda," *Izbr. soch.*, pp. 354-55.

26 Olesha, "Zametki, zamysly, plany," *Izbr. soch.*, p. 447. Another variant of the same fragment may be found in *Ni dnia*, p. 261. Perhaps it may be useful to the non-Russian speaking reader to know that there is no separate Russian word for *simile. Sravnenie* means both *simile* and *comparison.*

27 *Ni dnia*, p. 161.

compared do not fuse into one. The vehicle, the second half of the simile, is at least as present to the reader's mind as the tenor, the original pretext for the figure of speech. A multiplication of objects therefore occurs on the page, and may distract the reader's attention from the objects ostensibly being described. Olesha, however, does not wish to achieve a precise knowledge of the intrinsic nature of these objects. He merely wants to catch a fleeting resemblance—for example, the moment in *Envy* when a tugboat seems to Kavalerov to look like an almond. (p. 45)

In the second place, Olesha's comparisons usually incarnate only such momentary, *seeming* changes. This has led the critic El'sberg to declare:

> Each metaphoric association is granted only a very small interval of life, equal to the duration of a visual impression. Having played sufficiently with a particular object, Olesha leaves it in peace. [. . .] Machines, objects, people return to their real appearances and Olesha is already busy with new metaphoric toys.[28]

Temporary, illusory change is the kind Olesha uses most constantly. It is particularly characteristic of Olesha's short stories and, as we shall see, of the vision of Kavalerov, in *Envy*, who tends to look at things only long enough to establish *what else* they may be like.

In the third place, simile can underline not only resemblance, but also nonresemblance. Depending on the choice of the second element, the comparison may provide a real insight into the subject of the phrase. Or it may obscure it, by identifying it with something with which it has nothing essentially in common. Olesha's metaphors and similes are almost always based on immediately visible resemblances of shape, aspect, and color—resemblances of apparent form.

[28] Zh. El'sberg, "*Zavist'* Iu. Oleshi kak drama intelligentskogo individualizma," in his *Krizis poputchikov i nastroeniia intelligentsii*, p. 78.

A surprising number of these comparisons actually state that they are comparisons of form, as does the example from *Envy* just mentioned: "From this height, I saw instead of a tugboat something resembling in its form [*pokhozhe po forme*] a huge almond, cut in half lengthwise."[29]

Comparisons based on such superficial resemblances—and I take the term literally—may veil or violate the essence of an object, ignore or disguise its function. In one of his more abject apologies, Olesha discusses the consequences of his concern with formal resemblances:

Instead of the essence of a thing I see only its painted form. I cannot get to the heart of it. I am ill. The true world where form and content are joined does not accept me. I see only form. [. . .] Not long ago I wanted to compare a steamshovel to a giraffe. It looks something like a giraffe. But this is only a visual impression, an impression of form. And such a metaphor—a steamshovel as a giraffe—is a metaphor which speaks for the fact that the poet sees only the form and not the content.[30] The steamshovel should be compared with a hand. It is altogether different from a giraffe—it is the extension of human hands (and with the giraffe it is an extended neck). The steamshovel has the function of a hand reaching out. It is one of the hands of the giant, called Labor.[31]

Olesha's example of the giraffe is revealing. He cites it as an instance of his inability to make functional comparisons.

[29] *Zavist'*, *Izbr. soch.*, p. 48. MacAndrew tends to "clean up" Olesha's style by dropping from his translation the words *po forme* in the expression *pokhozhe po forme* [resembling in its form], and thus obscuring Olesha's insistence on this kind of comparison.

[30] Olesha tries to continue this partial perception from his childhood, when one could be happy because one didn't have to see the social meaning of *Robinson Crusoe*. He gives as another example illustrations in a volume of Pushkin. "We didn't understand the whole. We only saw separate scenes. A dwarf is flying through the air. The hero catches him." ("Pervoe maia," *Izbr. soch.*, p. 315.)

[31] Olesha, "Notes of a Writer," *International Literature*, No. 3 (July, 1934), p. 148.

Actually, it could very well be argued that the giraffe's long neck, which reaches out, does serve as the animal's hands. When Olesha has for once made a comparison which seems at least partially based on the similar functions of the objects being compared, he does not recognize the presence of the functional element. It is accidental. His intention was, in fact, to make a comparison of forms.

Of course Olesha is going somewhat overboard in his apology, and probably even the most rabid RAPP critic[32] would not demand the adoption of a uniquely functional standard for metaphor and simile. The giant of labor is certainly much duller and more commonplace than the giraffe. One cannot use only functional images in all cases, and no one but a RAPP critic would want a writer to do so. The important point, however, is that Olesha almost always uses a metaphor or simile which is nonfunctional if not antifunctional. If there is a system implicit in his images at all, the systematic element is the transformation of the object by the destruction of the reader's consciousness of its function.[33]

This is the inevitable result of the practice of seeing as if through innocent eyes. Only the fact that the perceiving sensibilities in an Olesha work are on a perpetual vacation makes such vision possible. The characters are free, like their creator—but unlike most of their fellow Soviet citizens—to "go to

32 RAPP: the abbreviated name of the Russian Association of Proletarian Writers; a group which maintained that all Soviet literature should serve, in form and content, the ideological needs of the Proletariat.

33 Olesha shares with the Serapion Brothers a preoccupation with deflecting the reader's attention from the "cognitive level" of the text. But for Olesha this is not merely an artistic method. It also fills a psychological need. The aesthetic impression achieved implies a rejection of the function. The point for Olesha is less to make a work of art in the process of which all things are deflected from the cognitive level of their existence (see Hongor Oulanoff, *The Serapion Brothers*, p. 33) than to deflect things from the cognitive level of their existence and, secondarily, in so doing, make a work of art.

the zoo any day they please."[34] The reader never sees them at work, and in fact most of them seem to have had very little experience of work, the most important aspect of a Socialist society. Berkovskii has understood the implications of this "holiday vision":

> In the illusoriness of such holiday contemplations, things obediently and willingly follow. [. . .] The universe unprotestingly bestows itself on the personal "I." [. . .]
>
> To pay attention in this way to external objects is but to continue self-observation. Only an idle perception leads to such a dissolution of external experience in the internal.
>
> The worker knows the *resistance of things.* He knows how to tame the universe.[35]

Olesha and his antiheroes have neither the patience nor the capacity for participation in *perestroika,* reconstruction, which demands a long struggle with material more resistant than language. They are interested only in *prevrashchenie,* immediate, effortless transformation. They imaginatively transform the world by seeing it in images, images which veil the resistance of things and the antiheroes' own incapacity to deal with them. Let us now consider in more detail how two of Olesha's antiheroes attempt to compensate for their inadequacy by imaginatively distorting the world and projecting themselves upon it.

[34] "My v tsentre goroda," p. 352.
[35] Berkovskii, "O prozaikakh," pp. 151-52.

Chapter II

The Need to Dominate and Control: The Problem of Envy

The recording sensibilities in Olesha's works very often feel helpless and inadequate, perceiving the world around them as malevolent and threatening. They then try to compensate for this actual powerlessness by seeing the world in a distorted and idiosyncratic fashion, projecting an imaginary control over it, and thus making it theirs. The mechanisms of this process of inadequacy and imaginary dominance, humiliation and revenge, are particularly clear in the short novel *Envy*.

Envy is one of Olesha's most successful works because, in his youthful confidence, Olesha maintains the distance between himself and his characters which is the sign of true artistic control. Nikolai Kavalerov and Ivan Babichev are completely created characters. Each has a distinctive perception of the world, and Olesha contents himself with working through them, subordinating his own presence to theirs. After *Envy*, Olesha seems to have been increasingly impelled to keep his reader constantly aware that he, the artist, was manipulating his characters. We shall see that the increase in visible control in these later works corresponded to a lessening of imaginative confidence, and therefore of artistic success. In *Envy*, however, Olesha still allows each of his antiheroes to try to cope with his surroundings in his own idiosyncratic way.

Nikolai Kavalerov, the Envious, the narrator through whose eyes we see the first part of the novel, is inadequate to the

Soviet world. He has little grasp of practical matters, and understands nothing when he looks at a column of figures. The verb *utilize* makes him cringe. He is not a producer, just a consumer. El'sberg calls him a "gourmand of observations," and Berkovskii notes that one of the reasons for the wealth of detail in *Envy* is a kind of epicureanism: "By transferring external objects into the sphere of personal consciousness, the impressionist, by that very action, prepares for himself an intemperate banquet."[1]

If Kavalerov accuses his benefactor, Andrei Babichev, of being a glutton, in his next breath Kavalerov serves himself up an even more incontinent feast by observing Babichev eat. Similarly, Kavalerov refuses to participate in a small supper to celebrate Babichev's creation of a cheap, nourishing salami. He prefers to remain an onlooker, enjoying his own "banquet" of impressions, since he feels a true, prerevolutionary artist—say Tiepolo—would never have stooped to paint "The Feast in the House of the Food Industry Manager."

Kavalerov cannot understand what can possibly be glorious in the creation of a new salami. He longs for a different fame, a different glory. He visualizes his wax double in a glass case, representing him down the centuries. He wants to be a Dick Whittington, a Lomonosov. But the middle period in the careers of these semilegendary figures, when "by fanatic efforts one reaches one's goal" (p. 39), always remains vague for Kavalerov. What he really expects is that fame will come to him of itself.[2] Such a transposition of cause and effect is typi-

[1] El'sberg, "*Zavist'* Oleshi," in *Krizis poputchikov*, p. 69; Berkovskii, "O prozaikakh," p. 152.

[2] Lidin (*Liudi i vstrechi*, p. 116) records that Olesha had great faith in chance himself. He wanted the kind of legendary fame that was Esenin's Gorkii's, and Shaliapin's. Olesha said about them, "None of them made any particular effort to achieve such fame. It came after them by itself." (*Ni dnia*, p. 146).

cal of Kavalerov. In particular, when he says, "Things don't like me," he really means, "I don't like things."

Olesha explained in "At Work on a Play" ["Rabota nad p'esoi"] that character may be defined in terms of one's attitude toward things.[3] Kavalerov's assertion "Things don't like me," is a way of avoiding responsibility for his inability to deal with things and for his fear of them. He explains away his feeling of being menaced by things as the result of persecution rather than a consequence of his own inadequacy:

> Things don't like me. Furniture tries to trip me up. Once the polished corner of some thing literally bit me. [. . .] If some piece of junk, a coin or a collar button falls off the table, it usually rolls under some hard-to-move piece of furniture. When, crawling around on the floor after it, I raise my head, I see the sideboard laughing. (pp. 26-27)

He knows he looks ridiculous, and finds in others the mockery that he looks for, or rather, that he assumes is already provoked by himself. Both the center of attention and the butt of ridicule in his own eyes, Kavalerov is always sure that people are laughing at him. He is therefore persecuted by his own doubts about himself, and by the hostility he consequently assumes must be directed at him by others.

Naturally enough, the things Kavalerov is least able to cope with and feels most menaced by are machines. He declares, "I don't understand anything about mechanics—I'm afraid of machines." (p. 101) His narration of a visit to the construction site of the Quarter [*Chetvertak*] (a mammoth dining hall where a good, nourishing meal will be sold for only a quarter) is a clear exposition of Kavalerov's relationship to the world of machinery. Seen from afar, "The construction site appeared to me a yellowish mirage hanging in the air [. . .] the separate

[3] Olesha, "Rabota nad p'esoi," *Izbr. soch.*, p. 411.

parts of the scaffolding fused into a distant, ethereal bees' nest . . ." (p. 54) Kavalerov, like Fedia, prefers to see from too far away to understand the real relations of things. As Kavalerov draws closer, the delicate image is replaced by an impression of chaos and noise which overcomes his senses. "I became deaf and cataracts formed in my eyes." (p. 54) In the same way that he did not understand Andrei Babichev's columns of figures, Kavalerov cannot distinguish the purpose of the activity around him. His senses serve not to comprehend, but only to escape the situation: "I began to walk along the wooden planking [. . .] the boards bent slightly, making me laugh, recalling childhood memories of riding on seesaws. I walked along, smiling at the way the sawdust fell, and the way it turned my shoulders grey." (p. 54) Such comparisons enable Kavalerov to abstract himself from his present situation to times of life when one is either too young or too old to exercise responsibility or be concerned with function.[4]

Kavalerov has come to the construction site to look for Andrei Babichev. He has finally climbed up almost to where the commissar is, when:

> [Babichev] flies by above me. Yes, he rushes past through the air.
>
> In preposterous foreshortening, I saw his immobile flying figure —not his face, only his nostrils. Two holes, just as if I were looking at a monument from underneath. [. . .]
>
> He was gone. He had flown away. On an iron waffle, he had flown off somewhere else. A crisscross shadow accompanied his flight. He stood on an iron thing which moved in a semi-circle, clanking and screeching. Whatever it was: some kind of technical device, a crane. A platform of crossed girders. [. . .] (pp. 54-55)

Babichev has flown out of reach by means of an uncompre-

[4] This feeling of having somehow jumped the period of full-blooded adulthood is one that Olesha discusses often; e.g., in "V mire," *Izbr. soch.*, p. 339.

hended, frightening, technical device; and Kavalerov, who has tumbled down to the accompaniment of the laughter of the workers, "smiles all around like a clown who has finished his performance." (p. 55)

Olesha through Kavalerov and others of his characters, formulated hundreds of comparisons which are inspired either by the character's incomprehension of a machine or by a desire to ridicule it and render it less menacing. He often animates machines. Turning a machine into an animal destroys both its essence—that of a nonorganic object—and its function. This corruption of a mechanical object by bringing it to life may indeed be a common device of the "technical grotesque" in literature,[5] but turning a machine into an animal does not necessarily make it more fearful. The animation of an object by means of a comparison may make it less threatening if the comparison is with an ineffectual, harmless creature. Certainly Olesha's comparison of the steamshovel with a giraffe works in this way. It is a kind of primitivism which gives souls to phenomena to make them more comfortable to consider. Then they can be dealt with on a personal basis and cajoled.

Sometimes when Olesha's characters corrupt the nature of artifacts by attributing life and will to them, the trick does boomerang and the objects get out of hand (as is the case with Ophelia, the feminine machine who turns on Ivan). Nevertheless, the object has been taken from Andrei Babichev's realm and then set back into the world metamorphosed into a form Olesha's heroes can conceive of, even if it is one they cannot always control.

The reverse pattern to Olesha's habitual changing of inani-

[5] Wolfgang Kayser, *The Grotesque in Art and Literature* (trans. Ulrich Weisstein), p. 183. There is, of course no doubt that Kavalerov's horror at the idea of Ophelia (a machine brought to life and imitating a human being) owes a great deal to a sensibility formed by the works of E.T.A. Hoffmann.

mate objects into animate ones is also present in his work. Such imagery is generally amusing and incidental. It does not usually deal with a situation of threat. In the romantic flowering hedge which is one of Valia's thematic associations, "A bird on a bough sparkled, jerked forward and clicked, making me think of a hair clipper."[6] (p. 43) Or all nature becomes a jewel to make the reader aware of the perfection of a moment in spring:

There are a few days in the spring when the trees which have just blossomed and the earth covered with grass give the character of an artifact to all of nature. Even a cloud seems artificial. [. . .] And if a shower should happen to pass over, one might think the rain had been planned to make the whole artifact look momentarily silver.[7]

Sometimes the mechanizations may seem frightening, but usually Olesha or his character is only amusing himself, the way children sometimes imagine monsters. The sketch "In the World" ["V mire"] is an exercise in this kind of imagination. Idling away part of a hot summer near Odessa, Olesha catches his foot in a stalk.

[. . .] dry and rough as an insulated wire, and I am afraid to kick it away as I don't see the beginning of the stalk and I can assume that a beam attached to the wire may collapse from the jerk—a beam which stands upright and which—if you get tired of amusing yourself with metaphors—is simply the grey, dusty trunk of a tree.[8]

This is a collapsing metaphor in two senses. Not only does it present an image of collapse, but the metaphor itself falls apart. Olesha kicks the props out from under it by reminding

[6] This is also a pun in Russian on the root: *strizh. Strizhka* is a haircut, and *strizh* is a kind of bird.

[7] Olesha, "Pervoe maia," *Izbr. soch.*, p. 316.

[8] "V mire," p. 344.

his reader that he is only being playful. Then he willfully induces a frightening optical illusion, just for the fun of it:

> My vision has taken on microscopic strength. I become Gulliver in the land of the giants.
>
> The insignificant, straw-like flower scares me. It's terrible to look at. It rises like the construct of some unknown, gigantic technology.
>
> I see powerful spheres, pipes, joints, elbows, levers, and the wan reflection of the sun on the stem of what had been a flower now seems like a blinding metallic gleam.[9]

There is, however, one kind of transformation of an animate being into an inanimate object which is always employed to reflect a character's real terror: when he sees another person as a mindless instrument of destruction. We read of Andrei Babichev: "He looked so terrifying that it seemed that he would step out and stride across the chauffeur's back and the hood of the car, smashing the barricade of their bodies as though he were a destroying pillar—as tall as the houses that lined the street." (p. 85) Because Andrei Babichev's ability to understand the significance of columns of figures and to control the real world appears to Kavalerov and Ivan to be a special gift, an occult power, they also see him as a priest, a witch doctor, a fakir who is everywhere at once. Kavalerov in

[9] *Ibid.*, p. 345. Aldous Huxley cites the similar vision of a girl ill with schizophrenia, for whom: "The summer sunshine is malignant, the gleam of polished surfaces is suggestive not of gems, but of machinery and enamelled tin; the intensity of existence which animates every object, when seen at close range and out of its utilitarian context, is felt as a menace." *The Doors of Perception*, pp. 107-8.

More generally, Olesha's use of "microscopic vision" probably owes a good deal to Zamiatin, who is reported to have said in an interview: "What is after all realism? If you examine your hand through a microscope you will see a grotesque picture: trees, ravines, rocks—instead of hairs, pores, grains, and dust. . . . To my mind this is a more genuine realism than the primitive one." Quoted in Struve, *Soviet Russian Literature 1917-1950*, p. 38.

particular sees him as a false god, a heathen, mechanical, frightening idol.

When Kavalerov is about to throw away the prototype of the wonderful new salami, the thought of Andrei Babichev stops him:

> I saw Babichev moving towards me, a terrible unconquerable idol with popeyes. I am afraid of him. He crushes me. He doesn't look at me, and yet he sees through me. I can only see his eyes from the side, because when his face is turned towards me, he has no eyes: there is nothing but his sparkling pince-nez, two round, blind little discs. He isn't interested in looking at me; he has neither the time nor the desire to do so. But I realize that he sees through me anyhow. (p. 49)

Kavalerov sees this dreadful, eyeless version of Babichev whenever he commits or thinks of committing a reprehensible action. At an important airport reception, he yells at Babichev that he is a "salami maker" and then: "Babichev's face turned towards me. For one tenth of a second, it remained turned towards me. It had no eyes. Only the two stupid circles of the pince-nez which gleamed like mercury." (p. 53)

Once more it is Kavalerov who projects onto the world the malevolence that he finds in it. Because he knows he is in the wrong, he cannot bear to meet Babichev's eyes. He therefore makes use of the sunlight to pretend that Babichev is a monster who has no eyes to meet.

Kavalerov then tries to flee into the semidelirious state into which he retreats whenever he cannot face the consequences of one of his acts, but the mechanical idol still follows him: "The terror of immediate retribution plunged me into a dreamlike state. I was dreaming. At least it seemed to me that I was asleep. And the most terrible thing in the dream was the way Babichev's head turned towards me on his immobile body, turning on its own axis, as if on a screw. His back remained unturned." (p. 53)

Andrei Babichev, both because of his power and because Kavalerov cannot stand being beholden to him, is the Enemy against whom Kavalerov has only the weapon of his imagery, his metaphors. To cover up his own inadequacy, Kavalerov indulges in an orgy of name-calling. He writes a letter "to take Babichev down a peg," which describes Babichev in a debasing way. Kavalerov's tirade enables him to see the idol as just a bloated piece of clay. Now it is Kavalerov who "sees through" Babichev, cuts him down, and has him "in the palm of his hand." (p. 57) In fact, Kavalerov controls the reader's vision of Babichev throughout the entire first half of the novel, allowing us to see the commissar only through the prism of his jealousy.

Kavalerov's envy of Andrei Babichev is expressed primarily through sexual and scatological imagery. As William Harkins has noted, *Envy* is pervaded by themes of castration and sterility.[10] Andrei Babichev is perceived by Kavalerov as a sexual threat. This is evident in the very first pages of the book. He is presented by Kavalerov in terms of immediate and overwhelming physicality. He snorts when he washes, and does setting-up exercises in his shorts: "His groin is splendid. A tender birthmark. A forbidden corner. [. . .] I have seen just such a mat, chamois-textured groin on a buck antelope. Amorous currents must flow through his office girls, accountants, and secretaries at a mere glance from him." (p. 26)

When Kavalerov feels sexually challenged, he turns his rival into a load of guts.[11] He carries out this procedure for Babichev

[10] William Harkins, "The Theme of Sterility in Olesha's *Envy*," *Slavic Review*, No. 3 (September, 1966), p. 444.

[11] Kavalerov calls the men accompanying a girl who laughed at him in a tavern a band of monsters and freaks: "You, freak number one [. . .] Your

in the very first sentence: "Mornings, he sings in the toilet." Kavalerov, lying in bed, imagines that he sees[12] the lit oval of glass in the bathroom door—itself located in the "bowels" of the apartment. Kavalerov interprets Babichev's little song for our benefit: "How pleasant it is to be alive . . . Ta ra! Ta ra . . . My bowels are resilient . . . ra-ta-ta-tara-re . . . My juices flow properly . . . ra-ta-ta-du-ta ta . . . Contract, guts, contract . . . tram-ba-ba-boom!" (p. 25)

Kavalerov surrounds Babichev with symbols of food and excrement. He tries to further degrade Babichev by a whole complex of images which tend to identify even the wonderful new salami Babichev has developed with bowels and intestines. The salami might be expected to impose itself as a symbol of Babichev's virility. But Kavalerov tries to overlay any positive masculine connotation the salami might have by identifying it with a system of excremental imagery: "From out of the mysterious incubators, swaying with the movement of its heavy trunk, came crawling a fat, tightly stuffed hose." (p. 48) The Russian noun is *kishka,* which means both hose and gut or intestine.

Kavalerov manages to make the commissar's attitude toward the salami seem obscenely hermaphroditic. According to Kavalerov, Babichev's breasts bob as he goes down a flight of stairs. Head of the Food Industry Trust, Babichev would like

face is like a harness. Your cheeks are pulled tight with wrinkles—not wrinkles but reins. Your chin is an ox, your nose a cartman, a leprous cartman, and the rest of you is the load on the cart . . . [. . .] You, who just laughed . . . do you have any idea how you laugh? You sound like an empty enema . . ." (p. 34).

[12] It is worthwhile noting that this description, like the descriptions of the murder and bathhouse scene in the story "Al'debaran," is an imagined description, i.e., the verbalization of something which the describer does not actually see. The detail must be ascribed to the construct of the imaginer, not to the actual scene.

to give birth to food [*rozhat' pishchu*]. He has already given birth to the Quarter, and the salami is also his child.[13] Like a mother, Babichev lovingly makes a bed for the salami on the table. Kavalerov then reverses direction: he sees Babichev as a bridegroom, in love with the degraded masculine symbol: "When Babichev held a piece of this hose in his hands, he became crimson, he even blushed with shame at first, like a bridegroom who suddenly realizes the beauty of his young bride and the enchanting impression she makes on the guests." (p. 48) Thus, Kavalerov mentally debases Babichev to help himself compensate for his own inadequacy.

Kavalerov's own sexual life is in fact a rather sad story. Although he dreams of a rare love, he sleeps only with the widow Prokopovich, symbol of his humbled masculinity, a slattern, forever entangled in the animal intestines which she cooks, and wielding a gleaming knife. Women scorn Kavalerov: "I call them and they won't come, the bitches." (p. 34) He does dream of a girl with a powdery laugh who slips into bed with him, but even then he is worried about how to reward her because, "Nobody has ever loved me for nothing. Prostitutes have always tried to get all the money they could from me." (p. 42) Reading his mind, the girl in the dream tells him her price is "only a quarter," once more linking his sexual humiliation with Babichev.

Kavalerov's insecurity is also reflected in various other ways. His immediate fear when he awakens the first morning in Andrei Babichev's apartment is that someone has cut his legs off while he was drunk. In general, as we have noted, things

13 Professor Harkins calls the salami "a repulsive parody" of a child. ("The Theme of Sterility," p. 447) It is that, of course, but one must note that Ivan, the father of Valia, and Kavalerov, whose mirror tells him, "you're cooked; produce a son," are capable of producing real children and not much else. As we have noted previously about "The Cherry Stone," in the context of Olesha's stories, a child of the loins may be considered inferior to the child of the artist's mind.

do not like him, and he goes around with sad little tails dangling where his jacket buttons should be.

It is not enough for Kavalerov to revenge his failures with women on Babichev. He must also find a way to protect himself against his successes—to flee the attentions of the widow Prokopovich. In her marvelously baroque bed, Kavalerov tries to return to a world of presexual innocence. He at first refuses to use the bed for any adult sexual purpose. He wants to use it as a child might, to act out daydreams of domination:

> If I were a child, Annie's little son, [. . .] I could have set up imaginary catapults on its barricades and opened fire on the enemy who would retreat over the soft, boggy ground of the blanket, leaving behind dead and wounded.
>
> I could have held receptions for ambassadors under the mirror arcs on the headboard. (p. 99)

He would have preferred a childish alternative to the sexual act:

> I could have set off on fantastic journeys along the carvings—higher and higher, up the legs and buttocks of the cupids, climbing on them as one climbs up a statue of Buddha, able to see only one part at a time and then, from the last arc, from a dizzying height, I would have slithered down the terrifying precipice, down into the icy abyss of the pillows. (p. 99)

True to form, Kavalerov prefers the satisfaction of imagined dominance: there he can still be king of the castle.

Kavalerov also has other imaginative techniques to recover control and achieve a feeling of dominance. Most of them depend on tricks of vision. He tries to perceive as one does in childhood: "Now I am an adult and can take in only the general outline plus a few details. Then I could . . . [. . .] Then neither distance nor scale nor time nor weight nor gravity [had to be] taken into consideration. [. . .] (p. 99) In childhood, one was allowed to play with one's vision.

Kavalerov still likes to play with his. For example: "The door was filled with shimmering summer darkness [. . .] (just such a tenderly chaotic darkness rises before one's eyes when one presses one's fingers against their closed lids) [. . .]" (p. 46) He likes to look through the wrong end of binoculars:[14]

I find that a landscape viewed through the wrong end of binoculars gains in brightness, clarity, and dimension. Colors and contours seem to become more precise. An object, while remaining a familiar object, suddenly becomes amusingly small and strange. This evokes images of childhood in the observer. It's just like dreaming. The odds are that a man, looking in the wrong end of binoculars, will break into a blissful smile. (p. 69)

Although the thought of seeing the world made miniature in this way does not cause Kavalerov to "break into a blissful smile," it does enable him to recover from a serious humiliation. Kavalerov has just been slapped. He first attempts to forget the indignity by thinking about a legendary swordsman who stayed dry in rain by cleaving the raindrops with his sword according to the stipulations of an inheritance. Kavalerov, however, is soaked to the skin. He finally regains his equanimity by thinking of the trick with the binoculars whereby the world is miniaturized while he retains his stature.

Kavalerov likes to miniaturize, and an even more satisfactory way to miniaturize and dominate than looking through the wrong end of binoculars is to look down from a height, particularly from a tower. Gaston Bachelard has described the joys of such domination as follows:

Du haut de sa tour, le philosophe de la domination miniaturise

[14] For a more exhaustive discussion of Olesha's playing with optics, see my 1961 Columbia Master's Essay: "Olesha: The Artist and the Transformation of Reality," or Nils Ake Nilsson's excellent article "Through the Wrong End of Binoculars," *Scando-Slavica*, XI (1965-66), 40-68.

l'univers. Tout est petit parce qu'il est haut. Il est haut, donc il est grand. La hauteur de son gîte est une preuve de sa propre grandeur. [. . .] La miniature est un exercice de fraîcheur métaphysique; elle permet de mondifier à petits risques. Et quel repos dans un tel exercice de monde dominé! La miniature repose sans jamais endormir. L'imagination y est vigilante et heureuse.[15]

This is Kavalerov's (and Olesha's) favorite state: solitude and domination in clear air and light, imagination freed.

Towers, with the possibility they provide for domination and the play they give to the romantic and metaphor-making imagination, are among the favored objects of contemplation in Olesha's works. Just looking at a tower from below enables him to inject a fairy tale element into humdrum reality.[16] "The Sukharev tower was beautiful, fantastic, rose-colored. Puss-in-boots might have walked on its battlements, and one might have seen him from the square." (*Ni dnia,* p. 139) Further, putting a clock tower in a description enables Olesha to mentally transfer himself from the ground where he is standing to the top of the tower itself. "As soon as one [a tower] appears in a description, it immediately brings in poetry, distance, height, a panorama. One might also speak of a stone tower, of the birds circling it, of the clouds beyond it, of the trees and the roofs below." (*Ni dnia,* p. 279) Olesha now dominates the trees and roofs, and the description leads off into one of those imaginary flights of liberation which I will discuss in detail in the following chapter. If there is no tower, a bridge will do as a point of dominating observation. Similarly, in any Olesha work, the most interesting thing about going to see a

[15] Gaston Bachelard, *La Poétique de l'espace,* pp. 160, 150-51.

[16] Typically, Olesha also likes to evoke towers which no longer have any function, for example, one near Odessa: "The tower's usefulness is long since finished. It has kept only its romantic properties: to dominate, grow black at sundown, throw a long shadow, and be flown around by flocks of martlets." ("V mire," p. 346).

sport played in a stadium is the opportunity it provides to look down from the grandstand.[17]

Just such a view from a distance gives Kavalerov two rare moments of well-being in *Envy.* He achieves a privileged vision, a special knowledge. One of the moments begins with a simple effect of perspective. Kavalerov is outside of and above a seemingly oppressed courtyard, "Kavalerov observed from above. To him, the little courtyard seemed to lack air. Everything which surrounded it, stretched out by being seen from an elevated vantage point, loomed over the little yard. It lay like a scatter rug in an over-furnished room." (p. 111) He has a secret knowledge of things which are above the eye level of someone on the ground. The change of perspective makes what he sees his: "The other people's roofs revealed their secrets to Kavalerov. He saw weathervanes in their real size and skylights whose existence no one down below suspected. A child's ball irretrievably lost when it had gone too high and rolled into the gutter. The antenna-spiked buildings retreated in stages from the yard." (p. 111) There follows an explicit example of Kavalerov's appropriation by vision. Not only the weathervanes and the ball are his, but also a drifting cupola: "The cupola of a church, freshly painted with red lead, happened to fill an empty spot in the sky, and it seemed to float until Kavalerov's eye caught it." (p. 111) Finally, Kavalerov can feel superior to another person because of the relative superiority of his position: "He saw [. . .] another observer, leaning out of a far-off window and either sniffing at something or eating it, who, in his obedience to perspective, was almost leaning on the trolley pole." (pp. 111-12)

After this moment of happy domination, Kavalerov refocuses

[17] See the fragment about a bullfight movie (*Ni dnia*, p. 176), the stadium scene in *Zavist'* (pp. 114-21, *passim*), and "Stadion v Odesse" (*Izbr. soch.*, p. 361).

on the yard and goes down from his elevated perch. Now Kavalerov's vantage point is one of inferiority. He looks through a hole in the wall which limits his field of vision instead of expanding it. He is spying. The sun burns his scalp as he watches the athletic Volodia do a high jump. Seeing Valia's bare legs, Kavalerov, now without tower, is seized by a "mixed feeling of shame and fear" and flees. (p. 113)

Kavalerov revenges another defeat—at the airport—by a characteristic appropriation and transformation of a menacing object. Having left the field, he stands on a green bank, "[. . .] leaning against a tree, with the wind blowing dust over me. I was surrounded by shrubbery, like a saint. I tore the tender, sour buds off the shrub and sucked them. I stood there with my pale, kindly face raised, and looked at the sky." (p. 53) He feels martyred, yet secure. Then his refuge is buzzed by a plane, probably the very one Andrei Babichev had come to see christened:

> A plane took off from the airfield. With a terrifying mewing, it banked above me, yellow in the sun, slanting like a sign board, almost stripping away the foliage of my tree. Higher and higher it went—I followed it, marking time on the bank. It sped away, now flashing in the sun, now turning black. It kept changing with the changing distance, taking on the form of various objects: a gunlock, a pocket knife, a trampled lilac blossom. . . . (p. 53)

Kavalerov has vanquished this menace by a progressive mental transformation of the airplane's form through changing distances. First he sees it as a gunlock (still threatening), then as a pocket knife (less so,) and then as a crushed lilac blossom. He has turned the latest triumph of Soviet military technology into a flower, a harmless blossom trodden under his own heel. Kavalerov has reasserted his control.

The ultimate tool for those Olesha heroes who desire to control and appropriate the world and turn it into their personal possession through tricks of vision is the mirror. The mirror first reassures them of their own existence. The mirror also gives one the power to project one's image—*my* reflection. In general the constant need to seek one's self in other objects, to superimpose one's self on them, and thus to acquire them, is all a part of the problem of mirrors—an assertion of the self which takes the form of a need to see one's self reflected, one of the central problems in Olesha's works.

Men of action do not need mirrors. The Commissar of War in *Envy* is reflected in the commotion caused by his presence. Andrei Babichev is reflected back to himself by the activity of his co-workers. There is a sentence in *Envy* which relates Babichev to a mirror. He merely puts on his pince-nez in front of the mirror, and then turns away. (p. 27) He is not even really looking at himself in the mirror. Once he can see, he pays no attention to his reflected image. He has no need of it.

Only Olesha's artists and dreamers need mirrors. The writer Modest Zand, hero of Olesha's self-justifying sketch "Something from the Secret Notebooks of Fellow-Traveler Zand," is aware that his attachment to mirrors is a sign of weakness: "It would never occur to some men to look at themselves in a mirror.[18] [. . .] Never to look in a mirror, never! Break oneself of the infantile habit of sizing one's self up. It's the characteristic of weaklings. A child in the bath investigates his hands, his feet, his little body." ("Koe-chto," p. 16) The mirror is, however, vitally linked with the only strength Zand has—his writing. "How passionately I dream of strength. I look at myself in the mirror very often. When I am working, I jump up and run to the mirror every minute or so." (p. 11) The dream of strength, the mirror, and the writing are all interdependent. The mirror implies not only introspection but also its corollary: projection of the self, and thus the creation of the personal imaginative construct which is a work of art.

18 "Koe-chto iz sekretnykh zapisei poputchika Zanda," p. 11.

Zand tries to look in every mirror he sees in the street, both to make sure he is there, and, by the same token, to dominate and take possession of whatever else may be reflected in the mirror at the same time. Sometimes catching a mirror may be like jumping a train: a rapid appropriation of a means of liberation. Zand says there are no purer mirrors than those carried in the streets by movers: "The mirror flies away. Swiftly it grabs up the house, the street lamp—I manage to catch my face which is flying off into the blue." (p. 11) He manages at the same time to dominate the things the mirror has "grabbed," and to join the flight into the sky.

Kavalerov too uses a street mirror to reassert himself after, as he thinks, he has been laughed at. He reaffirms his existence and power by means of the "special gift" which the mirror can bestow. In the mirror, the rules of the world are changed; the laws of optics and geometry are broken:

> . . . the natural force which determined your movement and made you want to go exactly where you did go is broken. You begin to think that you are seeing through the nape of your own neck, and, embarrassed by your special gift, you even begin to smile sheepishly at the passers-by. [. . .] A distance opens before you. Everyone is certain that it is a house, a wall, but you have a special gift: that's no house! You have broken a mystery: this is no wall, it is a mysterious world [. . .] (pp. 70-71)

Kavalerov is freed from the real world; he has induced an enchantment:

> You have, as they say, made a breakthrough. So unexpected is the breaking of the laws, so incredible the change in the proportions. But you rejoice in this dizziness [. . .] Your face hangs immobile in the mirror, it alone has kept its natural shape, it alone is a particle which has been saved from the regular world while everything else has collapsed, changed, and acquired a new regularity [. . .] (p. 71)

The viewer's special gift thus gives him a second reality, dominated by the one thing that remains from normality—the viewer's own face.

It is therefore appropriate that, at the halfway point of *Envy*, the two characters who want to dominate by imaginative projection should meet in front of a street mirror and continue their way together. Both Kavalerov and Andrei Babichev's brother Ivan have the same need to see their existence reflected onto the world. They both use illusion as their tool. Nevertheless, their methods of achieving their similar goals are quite distinct.

Ivan is bolder; he has more confidence in his imagination. Indeed, it might at first seem odd that Olesha stated it was Kavalerov, not Ivan, who saw the world with his eyes, as Ivan would appear to be the more impressive creative artist of the two. Ivan calls himself a modern magician because he tries to use illusion to impose his vision on the rest of the world. He has thought himself up (*"Ia sam sebia vydumal"*), and has invented a personage for himself: Ivan Babichev, prophet, leader of men. He has adopted a bowler hat and a pillow as the symbols of a "Conspiracy of Feelings," a crusade under his command directed against the Soviet power which he feels is crushing all those human emotions, both petty and exalted, which make life worth living.

Ivan is a master of florid oratory, unafraid to extend and overextend metaphors. For example, he apostrophises at length on the tree growing on the back of his hand, the system of veins which becomes more gnarled as he ages. He claims to have been an engineer, a man trained in understanding natural laws. He therefore affirms that he can control the things that frighten Kavalerov, such as dreams and machines. Ivan's triumph is the invention of Ophelia—an antimachine that laughs and cries and is tainted with all the pettiest human emotions. Ophelia is conceived as the weapon of Ivan's conspiracy. She is a blasphemy against Soviet society which, at least according to Ivan, idolizes the impersonal, emotionless efficiency of machines.

Ivan's attempt to impose his vision on the Soviet world is doomed to defeat. As he himself comes to realize, even his premises are false. Love and tenderness have not been banished. Even Valia, Ivan's own daughter, freely chooses the new world.[19] The last we see of Ivan in *Envy*, he has given up, and is more or less happily sinking into total vulgarity and indifference. In one version of *The Conspiracy of Feelings*, the play based on *Envy*, Kavalerov himself actually murders Ivan because he has turned out to be a false prophet.

The completeness of Ivan's defeat is a direct function of the boldness of his attempts to impose himself on the world. He wants to take physical revenge on people who have insulted him. He claims to have actually made a flower grow out of a mole on the chin of a nasty old lady, and suggests that Kavalerov revenge his humiliation at the hands of Andrei by killing the commissar. In the same way, Ivan wants people to believe in the actual existence of Ophelia, and declares that she will destroy Andrei and his new restaurant. Ivan, therefore, accepts no limitation on the sphere of activity of his imagination.

Kavalerov is more cautious. His aggressiveness remains verbal, and he keeps his revenge on the world within his own mind. He is aware of the limitations of the power of his imagination. In fact, he is made extremely uncomfortable by Ivan's insistence on Ophelia's physical existence. Kavalerov

[19] It was one of Ivan's and Kavalerov's major errors to assume that Woman belonged to the Old Era. In fact, she becomes the constant symbol of the new one. When the lovely woman in the bar laughs at him, the insulted Kavalerov returns to his table "carrying his beer mug before him like a torch." The woman who scoffs at him thus reduces him to his true standard, a beer mug. The crowning ingloriousness of it all is that Kavalerov gets his thumb stuck in the handle of the mug!

refuses to believe that the frightening whistle he had heard was Ophelia's: " 'Listen,' he said 'What nonsense! It was just a boy whistling between two fingers. I saw him. The boy appeared from behind the fence and whistled. Just a boy, that's all it was.' " (p. 103) Kavalerov does not like Ivan's fondness for ambiguity. He must know what is what at the start. Only then can he enjoy the contrast between what he knows really is and what seems to be. Kavalerov does not deny that there are limits. Most of the piquancy of his imaginative manipulations comes precisely from his knowledge that in imagination he can violate limitations of which he is fully conscious, but which he is otherwise powerless to change.

Ivan cuts his fantasy loose, maintaining that there are no boundaries between the world of his imagination and the Soviet world. He must therefore even face the prospect that if Ophelia is real she will turn on him, literally destroying her creator in her attainment of independent existence. In the end, Ivan does not even control Ophelia, and has no sphere of secure power at all.

Thus, if Olesha declares that it is Kavalerov and not Ivan who sees the world with his eyes, it is because Ivan's imagination is too arrogant. Kavalerov, by risking less, can salvage more. Claiming no real power over the physical world, he can delight his soul with imaginary dominance. Ivan invites destruction by insisting on the physical reality of his inventions. By so doing, he endangers those moments of fulfillment and illusory liberation which may be attained when the artist allows his imagination to play, more modestly, in full consciousness of the limits of its possibilities. Olesha is unwilling to risk such a loss.

Chapter III

Occasional Moments of Fulfillment and Liberation

From time to time the characters in Olesha's works do achieve moments of well-being and blessedness. Such moments of fulfillment are rare, fleeting, and always given a similar setting: one bathed in light and associated with clear air, bright colors, and unfettered movement.

Olesha's own image of an archetypal paradise is also of this kind. Characteristically, it is a literary image, linked to a myth of childhood as the source of all purity to which one longs to return. It is the image of the garden in H. G. Wells' "The Door in the Wall." The story concerns a government minister who once in his childhood had penetrated into a wondrous garden through a small door in a dilapidated wall. "There was something in the very air of it that exhilarated, that gave one a sense of lightness and good happening, and well-being. There was something in the light of it that made all its color clean, and perfect, and subtly luminous."[1] Everything was beautiful in this world, with "a warmer, more penetrating and mellower light, with a faint, clear gladness in the air, and wisps of sun-touched cloud in the blueness of the sky."[2] In this garden walked the ideal woman companion, and two velvety panthers played with a ball on the brilliant grass. (As Aldous Huxley has noted, the preternatural light and intensity of color of such

[1] H. G. Wells, "The Door in the Wall," in *The Country of the Blind*, p. 518.

[2] *Idem.*

a garden are characteristic of all Other Worlds and Golden Ages.)[3]

Occasionally in his later life, always at moments when he is going somewhere important, Wells' hero sees the door to the garden again, and passes by. The time comes, however, when the haunting memory of the beautiful garden makes his success tedious to him. One evening, he sees the door again and goes through. His body is found later in the deep excavation on the other side of the wall, but Wells' narrator implies that perhaps the hero really has found the garden after all.

Olesha finds in Wells' story a vocabulary of images parallel to that of his own happier visions:[4] the ideal feminine companion, the extraordinary clarity of colors, and particularly the penetrating light which infuses the objects in the garden. As the critic Gurvich has noted, "Everything near and pleasing to Olesha's soul immediately becomes associated in his consciousness with a lighting effect."[5]

Olesha loves all lighting effects, those produced by light bouncing off a surface as well as those produced by the absorption and containment of light. Surface light is laughing light, but real blessedness is usually represented by Olesha in terms of an object's or person's ability to absorb light, hold it, and thus possess it. Surface light is playful. It may distract a wayfarer, and "[. . .] if another dreamer takes our route, he will have the full pleasure of contemplating the famous bottle glass, those famous fragments celebrated by writers for their ability to flash unexpectedly amidst garbage and bleakness and create all kinds of mirages for the lonely traveler." (*Zav.*, p. 100)[6] Light brings out the color of objects. In fact, the striking

[3] Aldous Huxley, *Heaven and Hell*, p. 80.

[4] See *Ni dnia*, p. 226.

[5] A. Gurvich, *Tri dramaturga*, p. 146.

[6] Olesha is thinking particularly of Chekhov's famous broken bottle, glittering on a dam in the moonlight.

clarity of Olesha's color depends on the care he takes to bathe his imagined world in the peculiarly transparent atmosphere which he connects with the freshness of childhood: "I recognize in *Envy* colors which were noted by me in very early childhood, [. . .]"[7] says Olesha, recalling the clarity and brilliant colors of "transfer pictures," (black and white drawings which become colored when exposed to water). Coming out of the water into which they had been dipped, they had a special glitter like Moscow after the rain.

Olesha also likes to use rich, opaque colors: "In the pure air, the German eleven shone against the green field because of the bright, oil-paint colors of their uniforms. They wore orange, almost golden shirts with greenish-purple stripes on the right side of the chest, and black shorts. The shorts snapped in the wind." (*Zav.*, p. 115) Often, as in his reminiscence of a stable where his whole attention was devoted to the thick color of the horses' name plates, Olesha luxuriates in impasto effects. He constantly uses the Russian color verbs which also make colors more intense, such as the grass "greens." Green is one of Olesha's favorite colors, recalling the green expanse of airfields and playing fields seen in childhood. Green trees are opposed to inedible blue pears: nature is everywhere opposed to metallic artifacts.

Olesha declared himself to be a creature of the sun, source of all light. He was much taken with one of Mirabeau's last *mots:* that the sun, if not God himself, is at least His cousin,[8] and Olesha's memories of significant moments are marked, whenever possible, by the participation of this majesty. For instance, Olesha remembers that on the day of Tolstoi's death, "through the classroom windows, the shafts of sunbeams fell through the chalk dust [. . .]"[9] Or a carpenter is linked to the

7 "Talks with Readers," p. 77.

8 *Ni dnia*, p. 228.

9 *Ibid.*, p. 69.

sun, symbol of power, through his craft. And the odor of resin is yellow—as yellow as the sun.[10]

Not surprisingly, Kavalerov's picture of an idyllic life with Valia is filled with sunlight and brilliantly sparkling reflections in water: "[. . .] I visualize something different—a room somewhere, brightly lit by the sun. By the window there will be a bluish sink. The window will dance in the sink and Valia will wash at the sink, sparkling like a fish, splashing, running her fingers over the watery keyboard [. . .]" (p. 60) Valia, who represents Woman, is always associated with light. Her unexpected entry into a room affects Kavalerov like spherical lightning—a ball of light rolling into a space and filling it. She is always dressed in cherry blossom pastels (except on the one occasion when Kavalerov has a sexual vision of her: then she has on black shorts), because pastels represent pure desire and aspiration. Pastels are not opaque colors, but translucent, and Olesha loves the effect of light inside and *through* an object even more than light bouncing off one. Gurvich understood this when he remarked: "If Olesha were a painter, he would experience a tormenting difficulty in the choice of paints. Pastel, watercolor or oil [. . .] He would probably paint with translucent paint on glass, a work to be contemplated from bed, the sun lighting it."[11]

Moments of well-being are often associated with the sensation of the materiality of light: "You wake up early in the morning, the house is still asleep, the room is filled with sunlight. Silence. You don't stir so as not to break the motionlessness

10 *Ibid.*, pp. 37-38, 40.

11 Gurvich, *Tri dramaturga*, p. 115. Similarly, Ol'khovyi in "Eshche raz o literaturnom poputnichestve," *Pechat' i revoliutsiia*, No. 8 (1929), quotes D. Gorbov as saying that *Envy* is: "As though it were drawn on glass. If you put it on a dark surface, there's one picture in it. If you put it up to the light, you get something completely different, almost contrary in meaning." (p. 22) Olesha should have been pleased. He was in effect being compared to his beloved "transfer pictures."

of the light. There are socks lying on the chair. They are brown. But, in the stillness and brightness of the light, you suddenly notice in the brown material some separate, mobile, variegated strands, crimson, blue, orange."[12] Ivan and Kavalerov set off on a summer Sunday morning across an empty Moscow to see Valia:

Their walk could be described as enchanting. It took them through the holiday-deserted city [. . .] The slope up Tverskaia Avenue loomed blue. [color verb . . .] The light, unbroken by traffic, remained whole, as though the sun had just risen. So they were walking across geometrical patterns of light and shadow, or rather through a stereoscopic field, since the light and shadow intersected each other not only on the ground, but also in the air [. . .] In the space between two buildings, there fell a large mass of light. It was thick, almost dense, and it was no longer possible to doubt that light is made of matter. The dust carried around in it could pass for the oscillation of the ether. (p. 110)

For Olesha, light does not simply have the power to define and make visible other objects; it becomes itself a symbol of the fullness of living. It has a material existence as the substance at the heart of life. It is no wonder that the boy Ivan Babichev thought of blood not as a fluid but as light (p. 74), when Olesha can write the following dialogue with an unidentified person:

'From what can I create the future? The past has left glimmers, one can catch them, concentrate them, but the future. . . .'

He smiled:

'The future is still on the sun!'

He always returned to the theme of light. The material world is made of light. Call it what you will, quanta, atoms—it's light, it's the sun.

[12] "Vishnevaia kostochka," p. 267.

'Everything is made of the sun?' I asked.
'Of course.' (*Ni dnia*, p. 300)

He who possesses light controls everything it illumines, and life itself. The ability to concentrate and absorb light becomes the sign of grace. Conversely, those people who are not equal to life may be deprived of light. A gypsy can steal the day from Ivan and Kavalerov. The last light concentrates itself in the gypsy's bowl, and he walks away with the sun:

> The day was closing up shop. A bearded gypsy, in a blue vest and with painted cheeks, was carrying a clean brass bowl on his shoulder. The day was moving away on the gypsy's shoulder. The disk of the bowl was bright and blind. The gypsy walked slowly, the bowl rocked gently, and the day wheeled around inside the disk.
> The wayfarers stared after it.
> And the disk set like the sun. The day had ended.
> The wayfarers immediately turned in at a bar. (p. 89)

In Olesha's world, light tends to concentrate around the masters of life. Babichev's apartment is filled with light. Even the oval pane of opaque glass in the door of his bathroom becomes a beautiful egg the color of an opal when Babichev turns on the light. He has a vase of the finest porcelain, rounded, a tender, transparent blood red, like a hand held against the light. The rounder and more nearly perfect the object, the more light is attracted to it. Light is particularly drawn to buttons—for example, to those buttons on the pillow case of the bed Babichev has given Kavalerov: "Even mother-of-pearl pillowcase buttons came into my life, and in them, if you found the right angle, swam the rainbow ring of the spectrum. I recognized those buttons at once. They came back from a long forgotten, faraway corner of childhood memory." (p. 56)

The rainbow light in the round buttons of the pillow (a symbol of security and warmth of emotion, and therefore chosen by Ivan as the emblem of his cause), and the wonderful, dream-inducing bed combine in an image of blessedness given to Kavalerov by his benefactor.

Light also catches in the button of Babichev's drawers. It is a mother-of-pearl button "in which the pale blue and pink world of the room spins around." (p. 27) The life of everything in the room is thus concentrated on the belly of the Commissar of the Food Trust. It is not insignificant that buttons which can contain the world should prove uncooperative with Ivan and Kavalerov. The buttons of their jackets are lost, leaving just dangling, helpless tails. Even Kavalerov's collar button rolls away from him under the furniture. Sunlight concentrates in Babichev's suspender clips. Kavalerov has to hold his own suspenders closed with a pin.

The apple in "Liompa" symbolically holds all the richness of the world. It too is therefore a center in which light is concentrated and things collect: "There was an apple in the world. It was gleaming amidst the leaves, gently turning, and catching and turning with itself bits of the day, the azure of the garden, the window frame." (pp. 272-73)

Whoever or whatever is at the center where beams of light converge is also the center from which everything radiates. Olesha's characters, Kavalerov and Ivan, feel an anguished need to be that symbolic center. Everything must belong to them. Thence came the young Ivan's jealousy of a little girl who was the center of attention at a children's party: "She was queen of the ball. She did everything she wanted to. Everyone admired her, everything radiated from her and was drawn to her." (p. 92) Ivan had beaten her up and torn her dress, whispering "Don't take what might be mine." (p. 93) Once more the correlation between being at the center and possession is made clear.

While he beat her, Ivan still loved the girl. He compares this memory to his ambivalent feeling toward the rising new world: "Oh, how wonderful the rising world is! How brilliant the festival from which we are barred. Everything radiates from it, from the new era, everything is drawn in towards it [. . .] I love this world which is bearing down on me more than life itself, I worship it, and with all my strength, I hate it!" (p. 93)

As he cannot be the center of the new world, Ivan tries unsuccessfully to destroy it. Kavalerov's way of dealing with the situation seems more effective. His technique of possessing by seeing, of "catching with his glance" things belonging to the new world, things which he thus makes his, is precisely a way of placing himself in a radial center.

Given the connection in Olesha's imagination between possessing light and being oneself a radial center, a sun, it is not surprising that when his characters admit that they are not adequate to the new world they speak in terms of being blinded or going blind. Kavalerov thinks of himself as a blind man listening to fireworks when he cannot cope with Andrei Babichev's columns of figures. He says that cataracts form on his eyes when he visits the construction site.

When Ivan realizes that his revolt is based on a false premise and that all feeling has not perished in the new society, his reaction is a wish to go blind—so as not to be forced to believe his eyes:

> Valia, pluck out my eyes, I want to be blind [. . .] I don't want to see any of this: lawns, branches, flowers, knights, cowards. I have to go blind. I was wrong, Valia . . . I thought that all feelings had perished—love, devotion, tenderness . . . But it has all remained, Valia . . . Only, not for us. All we have left is envy, just envy and more envy. Pluck my eyes out, Valia, I want to go blind . . . (pp. 113-14)

Ivan expected the New World to be blinded by the glorious blooming of Woman in the dump hole of the Old World: "I dreamed of finding a woman who would bloom in the pit like an unprecedented feeling. Like the miraculous flowering of a fern. So that the new man [. . .] would be afraid, would draw back his hand, and close his eyes, blinded by the light of what he thought was mold." (p. 90) But Woman, tenderness, and love do not belong only to the Old World. The realization of his error incapacitates Ivan. "And so, the last dreamer on earth, I wander around the edges of the pit like a wounded bat . . ." (p. 90) which cannot see in the light of the new day.

In his analysis of certain French and German writers, Gaston Bachelard has described a kind of imagination to which Olesha's longings for light and liberation are very much akin: "Dans le règne de l'imagination, l'air nous libère des rêveries substantielles, intimes, digestives. Il nous libère de notre attachement aux matières: il est donc la matière de notre liberté."[13] Bachelard states that if one studies the imaginary union between what enlightens and what lifts up, one can show that it is one and the same operation of the human mind which carries us toward light and toward height. Indeed, Olesha's aspiration toward freedom is always expressed in terms not only of light, but also of unrestricted movement, and triumph over that most limiting of natural laws, the law of gravity. His imagination loves all manifestations of lightness (in both senses of the term), and weightlessness. Therefore, one of his central images of human liberation is the circus, where both body and imagination are loosed from the laws which limit everyday movement. There one may see people moving vertically:

[. . .] in the spectacle of a man moving vertically, there is an element of the most fantastic situation our minds can conceive of

[13] Gaston Bachelard, *L'Air et les songes*, p. 55.

> [. . .] when before our earthly eyes something happens which violates the law of gravity. [. . .] When something like that happens, for a second there arises before us the picture of some nonexistent world which has physical laws contrary to those of our world. [. . .] The circus has taken into account the powerful effect of all spectacles in which our habitual notions about the relation of man and space are destroyed. [. . .] Most circus acts play with balance: the tightrope walkers, the acrobats, the jugglers.[14]

Acrobats and tightrope walkers are the most fantastic figures in the circus. That is why Olesha's most cherished ambition as a boy was to become an acrobat: "[. . .] I had no inkling that I would be a writer. I wanted to be an acrobat. I dreamed of being able to somersault."[15]

As an acrobat he would achieve that personal, physical glory, the admiration of the crowd that he always desired. Later, Olesha recognized that there was an obvious link between his aspiration to be an acrobat and his career as an author: "Perhaps this dream of being able to do a somersault was also the first stirring of the artist in me, the first hint that my mind tended towards invention, the creation of something new and uncommon, towards brightness and beauty." (*Ni dnia*, p. 104) His awakening sensibility found the same secret fulfillment in the liberating images of the circus as it later did in the transformations of the world he performed in his writing.[16] What

[14] Olesha, "Zrelishcha," *Izbr. soch.*, pp. 350-51.

[15] *Ni dnia*, p. 104. He was even jealous of the prowess of others, commenting about a poster announcing the coming appearance of "The Boy Wonder": "Damn it, *I* am the Boy Wonder!" (p. 102).

[16] Olesha fell in love with a girl acrobat, enchanted by her lightness and the way her golden hair flew as she cartwheeled. Then, one day, he recognized her two male partners coming toward him with a pimply, unattractive youth who spat through his teeth. Olesha was crushed by the realization that the youth was the "girl" acrobat, and that the bright blond locks were a wig. Nevertheless, because it was the *image* with which he had fallen in love, Olesha affirmed that he loved the girl acrobat forever after. (*Ni dnia*, p. 106)

is his art after all, but a series of somersaults, the imaginative equivalent of the physical feat he could not perform?

Of course, the most perfect image of man's liberation from the shackles of the law of gravity is the dream of human flight. It is the image Olesha himself chooses to explain his whole life to his mother: "The only excuse is that all my life I have never been quite settled within myself. I always had a certain longing for something I couldn't define myself, a certain dissatisfaction. Somehow or other, I managed to tell myself that I didn't walk on the earth, but that I flew above it." (*Ni dnia*, p. 5)

From his childhood on, Olesha was obsessed with flying. He was the only one in his family who knew that Blériot had flown the Channel. Only he knew that Lilienthal had been killed, that a plane runs along the ground before it takes off, that the Voisins' plane was the one which most resembled a bird.

Predictably, among the few machines for which Olesha or his characters have any affection are "the melancholy bicycle which is like a dragonfly, transparent and frail,"[17] and the very early airplane which still resembled a bird with light, translucent yellow wings, rather than a heavy fish.[18] The interdependence of the early airplane and its lone pilot was Olesha's image of a humane technology: the alliance between a frail machine and the indomitable will of the hero who controls it. Olesha's mind was filled with images of the triumphal return of daring aviators:

I would have taught them to see the green field, the greensward of the first flights, lit by the young sun of the century, the empty, wonderful field and the crowd of people—officials in high hats,

17 "Zrelishcha," p. 350.
18 *Zavist'*, p. 31.

running among the daisies to meet the long shadow which slid under their feet. [. . .] Look, a transparent, yellowish, gleaming something or other, jointed [. . .] giving off a glitter of spokes, is landing on the grass.[19]

It is a curious fact that Olesha always envisages the landing and reception of the famous flier rather than the experience he must have had in flight. Olesha puts himself in the crowd, not in the pilot's seat. What he has to say about his own first flight is flat and uninteresting; only his feeling for the strong young men who are the pilots remains in one's memory from his sketch "The Flight" ["Polet"].[20]

Of course the airplane is a rationalization of man's desire to fly. The free dream is that of unaided human flight. As we shall see, Olesha very much admired his contemporary Aleksandr Grin's novel, *The Radiant World* [*Blistaiushchii mir*], which is about a man who could fly without wings. Olesha himself never allows his characters to fly (except in one special instance, which we shall examine later), but it is given to some of them to approach this state of absolute freedom more closely than others. Those who come nearest to flying without wings are the loved ones, usually incarnations of Woman as an ideal creature. Sometimes they are dancers, as is Suok of *The Three Fat Men.*[21] In any case, they are always young and light. As Nietzsche observed, everything that is good is light, everything that is divine runs on delicate feet.[22]

Valia has such lightness. "She was lighter than a shadow.

19 Olesha, "Ia smotriu v proshloe," *Izbr. soch.*, p. 286. As far as one knows (she is never described in detail), Ophelia is supposed to resemble one of these early planes.

20 Olesha, "Polet," *Izbr. soch.*, pp. 305-8.

21 Suok is opposed to a dancing master named One-two-three [*Raz-dva-tri*], a hack disciplinarian without a true dancer's free spirit.

22 Grin felt this too, and used the image of a girl running on the surface of the water as the master image and title of his *She Who Runs on the Waves* [*Begushchaia po volnam*].

The lightest of shadows, that of falling snow, might have envied her lightness." (p. 59) Her clothing is as light as she is, and a prey to the wind: "The pink dress, light as a shell, flew up about her legs, and Kavalerov saw how transparent it was. The wind blew the dress over Valia's face, and Kavalerov saw its contours outlined in the radiance and translucence of the material which was spread like an open fan." (p. 121) If Valia does not quite fly, in Kavalerov's dream she does float in the air, held up only by sound waves:

Valia was held in the air by the music coming from the instruments. The sound was carrying her. She rose and dipped above the trumpets according to the pitch and volume of the sound. Her ribbons were flying above her head. Her dress was inflated, her hair stood on end.

The last phrases tossed her up to the top of the stairs, and she fell into Volodia's arms. (p. 125)

Kavalerov's first image of Valia is all mixed up with clouds. She is leaning on a window sill, and "Clouds were moving across the sky and across the window panes, and their paths became entangled in the glass." (p. 44) That Olesha kept the image as a scenic direction in *The Conspiracy of Feelings*, the play he based on *Envy*, shows the association is not gratuitous.

Clouds are, of course, the traditional objects of pleasant reverie. Kavalerov does not play with them often because he can mold other objects to his imaginative will with almost equal facility. He does use them, however, in metaphors of ascension linked with the security of childhood dreams. Babichev's sofa becomes a "cloud bed": "From the height of your well-being, you lowered upon me a cloud bed, a halo that surrounded me with magic warmth [. . .]" (p. 56) Kavalerov's drowsing on the couch is a ritual of release and ascent: "By deliberate movements I provoke a ringing in the taut, new, virginal springs. The result is individual droplets of ringing, which rush up from the depths. I imagine bubbles of air striving to reach the water's surface. I go to sleep like a baby. On this couch, I fly back into my childhood. I am visited by bliss." (p. 40) Kavalerov directs this ascension. He is in control of a transformation of thought into dream substance:

Like a child, I once again command the tiny interval of time between the first change in the weight of my eyelids, the first blearing of the eyes, and the beginning of real sleep. Once again I know how to prolong this interval, enjoy it, fill it with the thoughts I want, and before sinking into sleep, still controlling my waking consciousness, I observe how my thoughts acquire the flesh of dream substance, how the bubbles of ringing from the submerged depths turn into rapidly rolling grapes, how a heavy bunch of grapes is formed, a whole vineyard, thickly entangled clusters of grapes, a path along the vines, a sunny road, and the warmth . . . (p. 40)

In this passage, Kavalerov attains the greatest fulfillment of which he is capable. He himself controls an orgasmic experience which is also more than that. It is an ascension into a world of sun, ripe fruit, and childhood warmth. All of Olesha's images of blessedness come together here. And we know that Kavalerov has found, for a moment, the door and his garden.

Olesha's story "Love," is the culminating work in his striving to write of liberation.[23] In a triumphant flight of fancy, Olesha employs many of his favorite devices to release the hero, Shuvalov, from his own Marxist will. Things change shape around Shuvalov. He sees the wrong causes for events and sees things that are not there. He passes through the state at the edge of sleep and dream. He loves; he flies. The story is a patchwork of impressions, and given the kinship of the various elements from which it is composed, the result is a

[23] Olesha, "Liubov'," *Izbr. soch.*, pp. 275-83.

summit of aerial romanticism, a paradise in constant change.

"Love" is about the transformation of the world. As Berkovskii has noted, what is really important in the story is not so much the girl Shuvalov loves as the fact that the world changes because he is in love.[24] The story's extraordinary lightness and humor are attributable to the fact that it is one of the few works wherein Olesha projects his vision onto an unwilling protagonist, one who does not need such a vision to justify his own existence, and indeed, does not want it. Olesha can therefore allow himself an almost absolute independence of imagery, as the transformations are not mediated by the psychic needs of the character. Shuvalov resists. He thinks of his problem as being one of a "correct" versus an "incorrect" vision of the world. When he succumbs, ideology yields to poetry, and his very struggle makes his final liberation a greater triumph for poetry.

The conversion of Shuvalov, who is faced with a transformed life, follows a definite progression. First, Shuvalov is placed in the situation of waiting: a helpless position which encourages idle observation. The initial step in romanticizing Shuvalov is made during his very first observation. He sees a lizard which can be spotted easily on a stone. It makes him think of something unlike itself, a chameleon which can change color and which would therefore not be visible. The first kind of change, then, is a change of appearance—color—which enables something to look like something else. This change does not *occur* in the physical action of the story, but merely as an idle thought. It does not seem to Shuvalov that the lizard *has* changed color. He merely conceives of the possibility that it could.

[24] Berkovskii, "O prozaikakh," p. 153. Viktor Shklovskii says substantially the same thing in his "Mir bez glubiny," *Literaturnyi kritik*, No. 5 (October, 1933), p. 119.

Next, he sees something which, to his literal sense, does not exist. It is the product of imagination exercised on real circumstances to produce a traditional liberating imaginative construct: castles in the air: "the architecture of the flight of birds, flies, and ladybugs, was transparent, but still it was possible to make out some sort of dotted line, an outline of arches, bridges, that deformed itself every second." (p. 275) Shuvalov classifies his observations. His orderly mind thus tries to defend itself against the intrusion of things which "do not interest him at all." He meets a color-blind man who sees everything but colors correctly. The color-blind man is not only deprived of the element of poetry, he also becomes the antipoet,[25] the possessor of a vision which deforms the world in the direction of dullness. He is condemned by his vision to eat blue pears. Shuvalov says he could never swallow such an unnaturally colored fruit.

Of course the choice between either Shuvalov's paradise or color-blindness is a false dilemma, as Olesha, intruding himself into the story, recognizes. Neither is "correct."

The branches with their club-shaped leaves were swaying. Shuvalov was standing in the middle of the path. The trees were rustling. She approached, welcomed by an ovation from the foliage. The color-blind man, who had taken the path to the right, thought: "My, it's windy," and he looked up at the foliage. The foliage behaved just as would any foliage agitated by the wind. The color-blind man saw swaying blue treetops. Shuvalov saw green treetops. But Shuvalov came to an unnatural conclusion. He thought: "The trees are greeting Lelia with an ovation." The color-blind man was wrong, but Shuvalov was even more wrong. (p. 277)

Here Shuvalov is ascribing a false cause to a real event.

[25] He is a negative double of the Artist. For as the Serapion Nik. Nikitin said, "The Artist always suffers from a kind of color-blindness." ("Vrednye mysli," *Pisateli ob ikusstve i o sebe*, pp. 117-18.)

When Shuvalov shakes Lelia's hand, the world suddenly changes at the contact. Olesha claps distorting lenses on his unwilling hero. "Why are you screwing up your face?" she asks. "It seems as though I were wearing glasses," he answers. (p. 277) The first miracle that occurs in this changed world is that a slender, bright little tree, an enchanted umbrella, springs up where an apricot stone falls. Shuvalov is no longer bound by time—he need not wait for five years for a tree to grow. He is freed to live in the world he imagines, where thoughts materialize.

Shuvalov takes the next big step toward liberation during the night, when he sleeps with the girl with whom he is in love. Lelia is young and light, but she is also linked with the image of fruit rather than that of flowers. She dribbles apricot juice. In Olesha's system of images, she is therefore accessible as a woman.

Later, Shuvalov is initiated into the "second existence of things," revealed only in the few minutes before falling asleep:

> Suddenly coming closer, parts of the wallpaper patterns grew larger, became more detailed, and changed. At the edge of sleep, close to childhood sensations, he made no protest against the transformation of familiar and lawful forms, especially as the transformation was touching: instead of spirals and rings, he saw a she-goat, and a chef. [. . .] "And a chameleon," he said, falling asleep. (p. 278)

Love and drowsiness lead Shuvalov to accept this second existence for things. During the night the transformation of the world which had begun on the day of their meeting is completed, and Shuvalov awakes on a new earth. It is a blissful world where the old laws are finally broken, and everything is touching and funny. As a sign of blessedness and sexual security, his buttons button themselves. In the sun's rays,

Lelia's dresses are as iridescent and light as Mongolfier balloons.

Shuvalov is careful, for he fears he has been granted the power of materializing thought. He tries not to think of a tiger, and then perceives a striped, bloodthirsty wasp which flies in the window as the approximate materialization of his half-formed thought.

Then Shuvalov flies. He flies because he is the happy lover. His flight is the ultimate sign of his release from laws and his conquest of the new world of love.

Shuvalov's Marxist conscience is not at rest, however. That afternoon, waiting in the park for Lelia, he dreams of Isaac Newton. Newton, of course, is the representative of all the pedestrian laws Shuvalov has broken.[26] In the dream, images from earlier in the story are picked up and form echoes which give the story structure. Newton's apple tree, for instance, picks up the theme of lightness, which harks back to Lelia's dresses and her own fragility. Thus, Newton's tree, which is usually linked with the discovery of the law of gravity, here becomes linked with flight and with liberation from that law: "The frame of the apple tree, the skeletal frame of its crown, light and fragile as the frame of a Mongolfier balloon, showed through the scant cover of its leaves." (p. 280)

Later, Shuvalov discusses his problem with the color-blind man. Shuvalov is a Party member, yet he is living in paradise and is forced to witness what he calls a "criminal, unscientific perversion of matter." (p. 282) The color-blind man refuses to trade corneas and, therefore, disabilities with Shuvalov.[27]

26 Newton is interested in binding laws—those of optics and gravity—and in problems of mechanics. He has long been among the poets' favorite symbols for the singleness of vision which is destructive of creative energy and imagination. Blake, for instance has Newton right up with Nobodaddy in his deadly, old man's heaven.

27 Olesha is characteristically unconcerned with the medical fact that color-blindness is not caused by a defect of the cornea.

Shuvalov finally finds Lelia asleep in a bower. The color-blind man comes upon them, and seeing Lelia, changes his mind and offers to trade his corneas for Lelia's love. But Shuvalov's conversion is now complete. He says, "Go eat your blue pears." Shuvalov has opted for paradise.

Chapter IV

The Limitations of Olesha's Imagination

The critical view of Olesha as a fundamentally lighthearted, whimsical writer who allows his fantasy to run unfettered through the world, transforming everything it touches, rests on stories such as "Love" and on the fleeting moments of liberation achieved by Kavalerov. Even in these early works, however, Olesha traps his characters. They can be no freer than the imagination which created them, and Olesha carefully, deliberately, anchors his fantasy to earth. Even Shuvalov's wings are clipped. If "Love" is the work which affirms most strongly the validity of a vision which seems able to transform the world, it also clearly delimits the boundaries of Olesha's imagination. The transformations are only momentary, illusory, even there, in the Land of Love.

Olesha has chosen "love" as the transforming circumstance precisely because it is so well worn, and it therefore allows him both to use and to parody an old convention, even to the extent of playing on the clichéd language of love. This clever reference to clichés can be limiting, as Shklovskii noted when he reproached Olesha with "seeing things in quotes."[1] Quotation and playing on words deflect the reader's attention from the story to its writer. Shuvalov, for example, *does* fly, but is immediately weighed down again by the reader's consciousness of the writer's presence, a presence which must limit the world of created fantasy. Shuvalov's flight, the central symbol of liberation, is the materialization of a cliché, a metaphor

[1] Shklovskii, "Mir bez glubiny," p. 120.

taken literally: "[. . .] not feeling the steps beneath him because of his happiness, Shuvalov got downstairs and went out into the courtyard . . . Yes, he didn't feel the steps. Then he didn't feel the porch or the sidewalk. And then he discovered that it was no illusion but reality, that his feet were hanging in the air, that he was flying." (p. 279) So far, the image is independent and unqualified by explanation, as is the figure of Grin's flying man in *The Radiant World.* But then Olesha plays with language. By explicitly bringing in a cliché, he makes the reader notice that there is a linguistic "frame" around Shuvalov, and in effect grounds him in the reader's mind: "[. . .] that his feet were hanging in the air, that he was flying. 'Flying on the wings of love,' somebody said inside a window as he passed." (p. 279) Olesha therefore uses the reader's consciousness of language as a limiting frame; his deliberate laying bare of the poetic device weakens the realized metaphor, and insures that the story remains on the level of poetic irony. Shuvalov, even in his moment of triumph, is not allowed to soar in completely unfettered fantasy.

Elsewhere, however, Olesha denies that he is one of those writers who use the reader's consciousness of the devices of language as a limiting frame:

There are two kinds of writers. One kind in whose productions you can see how the thing was written, see its structure. And there are others in whose works you do not note the language as you read, but see only those pictures which are described by the language. Let us suppose that you look out of a window and lean right forward; then you do not see the window—the window frame and the sill—you see the fields and the sea. Or you can look so that you do see the window. [. . .]

When I write, I think only of how to transfer what I see with the maximum of vividness. I want the reader to look at the world which I show him and lean right out without being distracted by the window frame and things standing near the window.

> One reader told me that he does not know what my sentences are like, long or short. "I see what you show me and do not notice the methods you adopt to make me see."[2]

This statement is troubling. It is doubtful that even an unsophisticated reader can miss seeing Olesha's devices; certainly a trained one cannot help doing so. Further, Olesha is deliberately placing himself among those writers Shklovskii had earlier called "translators":

> There are two attitudes towards art.
>
> One considers a work of art to be a window open onto the world. It wants to convey, through words and images, something which is behind them. Artists of this type should be called *translators*.
>
> The other attitude towards art considers it to be a world of independently existing things. Words, relationships between words, thoughts, the irony of thoughts, their discrepancies, these are the contents of art. If one compares art with a window, then it can only be a false one, a picture of a window.[3]

It would be easy to dismiss Olesha's comment as deliberately disingenuous. Surely Olesha is fully conscious of the pervasiveness of the artist's presence in these stories. Does he, despite what he says, consciously put a frame around his stories for the delight of other writers who watch Olesha *doing* the story rather than what happens in the story itself? Or is the visible frame really a weakness which he would like to overcome?

On the one hand, it is obviously the "writtenness" of Olesha's works that accounts for their particular charm. For Olesha, language is in fact part of the object to be viewed, and therefore, one is constantly aware of the presence of the author, the wielder of language, through the fabric of the work. Thus, even in his earlier stories, Olesha is not content to entirely

2 "Talks with His Readers," p. 79.

3 Viktor Shklovskii, *Zoo: pis'ma ne o liubvi*, p. 83.

efface himself and leave his imaginative construct to stand free, unhedged about. On the other hand, it is clear from numerous comments that he most admires those artists who *can* efface themselves so that the reader forgets that what he is reading has been invented by someone. Olesha explains H. G. Wells' superiority over Jules Verne in these terms: "When we read Jules Verne, we never forget that it is all invented; reading *The War of the Worlds,* for instance, we suddenly fall under a spell: it suddenly begins to seem that there really had been a Martian attempt to conquer the Earth."[4] It is precisely this ability to make the unreal seem real which Olesha envies in Wells, Grin, and Aleksei Tolstoi. He bows before the "authenticity" of Aleksei Tolstoi's invention, which is not hedged around by a compulsion to explain away or undercut: "As soon as I think of A. Tolstoi, pictures of the world he created rise up one after another before me, so authentic, so real, that it never occurs to one that it is made of lines of print. No, it exists; there it is beside me! [. . .] A man who creates an imagined but authentic world, an artist of genius is here before me."[5]

Olesha feels himself incapable of this "authentic" invention. He can make literal things happen fantastically, but he cannot make fantastic things happen literally, because the latter achievement demands a real grasp of the functioning of the world, a grasp of how things actually do happen. Wells, therefore, makes one "live in a fantastic environment as if it were the real world."[6] Reading Olesha's work, one watches a char-

[4] *Ni dnia,* p. 227. One must be careful to distinguish Olesha's two uses of the word "invention" [vydumka]. Although he usually employs it as a term of praise to denote the highest kind of literary production, he occasionally uses it as he does here, in Lev Tolstoi's more derogatory sense of "It's all made up."

[5] "Vstrechi s Alekseem Tolstym," pp. 397-98.

[6] "Talks with His Readers," p. 80.

acter live in the real world as though it were a fantastic environment.

I do not mean to imply that Olesha's works are therefore less brilliantly successful in achieving what they intend to. Nevertheless, they do set out to create a world of fantasy, one of whose primary objects is to show the reader the artist's constant control over it. Olesha's works therefore remain more exercises of the Fancy, to use Coleridge's distinction, than creations of the Imagination. Imagination is dangerous; it may lead into unknown directions and depths. But by exercising his Fancy, the artist may block out the claims of Imagination and remain secure in his control of a surface beyond which he chooses not to penetrate. It is Fancy, not Imagination, which is the "Beloved of Reason."[7]

The need for the safety of constant control also helps to explain the at first surprising distrust of dreams visible in Olesha's works. Although dreams are a traditional source of liberation, Olesha himself admits to being afraid of them, precisely because they are usually beyond his conscious control. He is troubled by the independence of dream visions: "Isn't it amazing that strange visions should appear in our minds. Why does it happen? Who has volunteered to frighten us? Is it possible that nature knows what we fear and what we don't? Does our conscience scare us? Or is it an atavism, a memory of the sabre-tooth tiger?"[8]

While Olesha may be master of his waking thoughts, a dream can force him to consider the unknowable:

Sometimes you've barely closed your eyes, when suddenly a vision invades your still sleeping brain—no, not a vision, but some terrible line, even, perhaps a phrase. . . . You experience a second of

[7] *Zavist'*, p. 77.

[8] Olesha, "Iz zapisei 'Ni dnia bez strochki,'" *Izbr. soch.*, p. 482. This passage and the one which follows are from the same page of *Izbr. soch*, but are absent from the final edition of *Ni dnia bez strochki.*

incomparable fear. But is it really fear? No, it's already nonexistence itself. It's the effect on the brain of the activity of certain cells which have begun to work, probably by accident, and which will be called upon to function only after death.

Such dreaming moments threaten Olesha with an unimaginable future and an unthinkably distant past: with a world independent of his conscious definition of it.

His characters also feel dreams as threats. Daydreams are more tractable. In fact, Olesha's heroes much prefer daydreams to dreams. What Kavalerov likes best is not the dream which comes to him in deep sleep, but the dream which occurs just at the edge of sleep, which I have already discussed. He prefers it precisely because it is brought about by the initial exercise of a conscious control.

It is true that even Kavalerov does sometimes have recourse to dream. When he has overstepped the bounds of the permissible, he attempts to retreat into a self-induced, hallucinatory state in an attempt to convince himself that the dreadful situation is only a dream. When, at the airport, Kavalerov has shouted "salami-man" at Babichev, he tries to hide, and says, "The terror of some impending retribution plunged me into a dream-like state. I was dreaming. At least it seemed to me that I was asleep." (p. 53) Kavalerov hopes that if he is asleep an effort of will can enable him to awaken and dismiss a situation over which he has lost control. He makes a similar unsuccessful attempt after he has indulged in his drunken tirade at the bar: 'I was horrified at what I was saying. I vividly recalled those peculiar dreams where you know that you are dreaming, and you do whatever you want because you know that you are going to wake up. But in this case, it was clear: no awakening was to follow. The skein of irreparability was frantically winding itself taut." (p. 34) Escaping into dream never really works.

Furthermore, real dreams may force one to recognize unpleasant truths which, awake, one could keep from one's conscious mind. Kavalerov is brought to the final realization of his own worthlessness through a dream and purgatory illness which occur in the novel's last pages—an obviously Dostoevskian technique. Kavalerov is naked, save for a blanket. He gleams like a lizard—the lizard which in Ivan's terminology is the heraldic symbol of Envy. Thus garbed, Kavalerov watches Valia float through the air into Volodia's arms.

Kavalerov's refusal to see this defeat calls up a defense—Ophelia, the machine who is supposed to revenge Ivan and Kavalerov on the New World. But instead, Ophelia strips him of his blanket, and he is naked, even more sexually humbled than he was by the mere fact of seeing Valia go to Volodia. Then Ophelia pins her squealing creator to the wall with a shining needle.[9]

Thus, Kavalerov is forced to see Ivan destroyed and himself exposed. Volodia gets Valia; the Quarter rises, beautiful, transparent, not oppressive. Kavalerov's illusions have been destroyed, and he recants. He awakens, determined to apply what he has learned from the dream to his life, but cannot. Powerless to change himself, but with illusions gone, only indifference remains to him.

Indifference is also the result of an attempt made by Kozlenkov, the hero of "The Prophet" ["Prorok"],[10] to integrate the significance of a dream into his everyday existence. "The Prophet" also testifies to Olesha's limited faith in dreams. Unlike his contemporaries, the Surrealists, he did not believe dream could penetrate daily life and become an integral part

9 Olesha seems to have borrowed this scene from *The War of the Worlds.* In *Ni dnia,* Olesha recalls it: "[. . .] *War of the Worlds,* a novel in which there is a scene where a dismayed man in a jacket, and a tie which is all askew, rooted to some pitiful urban wall, watches in horror the steel tentacle of a Martian approaching him through the ruins. . ." (p. 226)

10 Olesha, "Prorok," *Izbrannoe,* pp. 75-82.

of it. In his work, dream is presented as an alternative to life, not an enrichment of it.

"The Prophet" begins within a dream. Kozlenkov is alone on a hill in a dry, bright immensity. An angel approaches him:

Along the twisting dirt path which led up the hill to Kozlenkov's perch, an angel approached swiftly, an enormous angel with black hair curling to his shoulders. He was powerful and had no wings. He wore a dressing gown of a red, dark material; there was a staff in his hand. Beneath the dressing gown, his knees moved circularly. [. . .] The tall staff with flowering bright green buds thumped the dry earth between the blades of grass. The staff gleamed as furniture gleams. The buds looked like the heads of nestlings . . . (p. 75)

The angel lays his hand on Kozlenkov's shoulder in a kind of annunciation, and Kozlenkov wakes up.

On his way to work, Kozlenkov watches a young girl, an attempted suicide, being carried from a neighboring house. He realizes that the girl was unhappy, abandoned, starving. Suddenly he notices a dark window which he knows has not been opened since the past winter. Then he notices a senile old woman on a porch. " 'Misery,' thought Kozlenkov, 'ah what misery.' And he began to be sorry for everyone." (p. 76)

Kozlenkov is a maximalist. He feels something must be done to vanquish all human grief at once. He could say with his creator, "The major characteristic of my soul is impatience."[11]

Kozlenkov didn't have the power to overcome human unhappiness at once. He knew there was no such power. One had to wait, to gather up enough strength.

But Kozlenkov's desire was so strong [. . .] he couldn't stand even a moment's wait. Therefore he thought of a miracle.

"One ought to perform a miracle," he sighed. (p. 77)

[11] *Ni dnia*, p. 11.

At lunch, remembering the dream, Kozlenkov imagines himself performing the miracle which would destroy unhappiness. A simple laying on of the hand suffices:

> [He visualized the picture of himself] entering the yard with a flowering staff. [. . .] He touches the girl's brow with his hand. Instantly, the double window [. . .] flings itself wide to the air and sun [. . .] the wind blows the curtains. . . . Instantly, youth returns to the old woman, her son returns. (p. 77)

Up to this point, the structure of the story is fairly simple. There is a dream, and then a daydream which incorporates certain characteristics of the dream. Both exist within the mind of Kozlenkov. But Kozlenkov decides to perform a real miracle. As he walks through the rooms of his office opening doors, he creates a draft—often the accompaniment of power.[12] One door shuts behind him with a bang and at the same time the next opens by itself.

> Most important, he saw that all their heads were bowed [. . .] Of course he knew it was because of the draft. But he also saw that no one could raise his eyes to him. And he could give this any meaning he pleased.
>
> He thought, "They have all bowed down before me. I have seen an angel. I am a prophet. I must perform a miracle." (p. 78)

People shout at him because the draft is blowing papers off the desks, "but it was not forbidden for Kozlenkov to give the cries another meaning."

Here Kozlenkov is trying to insinuate his dream into the real world. He does so by ascribing false causes to real effects. Nevertheless he *does* perform a miracle. He gets a two-week advance on his salary. Everyone cries "miracle, it's a miracle." It is, of course, a rather low-level miracle, a practical miracle and not the moral miracle Kozlenkov demanded. But even if

12 The Commissar of War in *Envy*, for example, also creates a draft by his passage.

he has not brought an end to all human suffering, he does now have the means to buy the girl something to eat. Possibility and impossibility are becoming intermingled. Kozlenkov heads toward the hospital with the money. On the way, he is attacked by a man who thinks he is to blame for the girl's attempted suicide. Kozlenkov thus takes another man's fault upon himself, and even acquires a crown of thorns while rescuing a child's ball from a shrub.

But at this point Kozlenkov begins to understand the sources of his dream. He sees the apron of a gardener blowing about his feet like the drapery of a marble angel. The crown falls from Kozlenkov's head; he is discomfited and can no longer be a prophet. When he returns home without seeing the girl, he recognizes other sources of his dream images. As he had done the night before, Kozlenkov buys an onion from a powerful laundress, dressed in red, selling cabbages with curled leaves. He eats it for supper, and again is tormented in his sleep by thirst and heat. Again he sees the angel climb toward him. A physiological explanation is given: at the very second when the dream begins, so does heartburn. When he awakens, Kozlenkov understands the causes of his dream and the sources of its images. He is therefore freed from it; it is explained away.

The explanation enables Kozlenkov to regain his peace of mind. When he recognizes the ways in which his angel resembles things he has seen in his daily life, the power of the dream is destroyed. The original moral impulsion to create a miracle, to relieve human suffering, is gone too. Moral concern is linked to the capacity to deal with things in pure imagination. Kozlenkov feels unable to handle a single case of unhappiness. He must change the whole world immediately—a thing which is impossible. He therefore becomes indifferent.

The pattern of the prophet who goes from grandiose hopes to indifference parallels the decline of Ivan Babichev, also a self-styled miracle maker. The despairing reliance of Olesha's heroes on miracles which never work out is a reflection of the fact that they as individuals do not have the patience to work for a desired result, that they must have an easy way, outside the normal laws of cause and effect, to attain what is otherwise impossible at a given moment.

It is also an analogue of a dilemma which plagued many of the more complex members of Russian society during the first generation of Soviet rule: the insufferable split between what was desired and what could be achieved. Society for the first time was committed to changing life. But this change, not being miraculous, had to be mediated by industrialization. Before everyone could live decently, at least one generation would have to live in drabness and want. "The Prophet" represents the despair of the imagination before the limitation of one's real capability.

There is, however, a literary genre in which the writer may be entirely free from the limitations imposed by possibility, if he so wills. This genre is *skazka.* "Fairy tale" is a somewhat misleading translation of the Russian word which designates a broad spectrum of tales in which there are strong legendary or folk elements, but not necessarily supernatural beings. I shall therefore keep the Russian term when the English "fairy tale" would be particularly inappropriate.

Olesha considers *skazka* "the most amazing, tender, and simple thing in literature,"[13] a genre which demands a genuinely childlike perception admitting of no falsification.[14] Yet, not even in the writing of *skazka* does Olesha allow his imagination to play completely unfettered. Even in *The Three Fat Men* he does not permit the "impossible" to happen.

The Three Fat Men, a brilliantly colored adventure story theoretically intended for children, tells of a revolution which takes place in a land ruled by the Three Fat Men who own,

13 "Literaturnia tekhnika," p. 433.

14 "Pervoe maia," p. 313.

respectively, all the grain, coal, and iron. The country is divided very simply into the rich, who support the Fat Men, and the revolutionary poor, aided by the circus performers and an extremely learned scientist, Doctor Gaspar Arneri. The Doctor, the tightrope-walker Tibul, and a girl circus performer who pretends to be a wonderful doll, manage to free the revolution's leader, the gunsmith Prospero, from the cage where he is held prisoner in the Fat Men's palace zoo. All join in the final triumph of the people over the tyranny of the gluttonous Fat Men.

It is not surprising that Olesha should have turned to *skazka* as a way of simplifying the Revolution. He once stated: "People [such as Andersen, the Brothers Grimm, and Hoffmann] who can transform complicated social processes into a light and transparent image seem to me the most amazing poets."[15] *The Three Fat Men* enabled him to write a positive work about the Revolution without requiring him to have any real knowledge of its dynamics.[16] At the same time, it was an attempt to pre-

[15] Olesha, in his introduction to Igor Moiseev's ballet adaptation of the work: I. Moiseev, *Tri tolstiaka*, p. 8.

[16] The critic Gurvich accuses Olesha of using the revolution simply as a Christmas tree on which to hang balloons, stars, and other decorations. He takes the traveling theatre in which Suok works as an analogue of the whole fable. The theatre is called the "Gay Box". It wanders in a country called the "Long Shadow." Gurvich sees in *The Three Fat Men* an attempt on Olesha's part to take to his heels before the "long shadow" of reality, and to conceal himself from it in the "gay box of art." (*Tri dramaturga*, p. 123.)

It is true that the heroes of this revolutionary fable are a marginal lot, with not a proletarian among them, save the gunsmith Prospero, who spends most of the time in a cage. The active characters, besides Dr. Arneri, are all circus performers and actors. The hero is an acrobat, the heroine a dancer.

We have already seen the connection in Olesha's mind between circus performers and liberation. It is imaginatively logical that his liberators be acrobats. The circus is, however, a spectator sport. The audience sits and watches others do death-defying feats. A revolution is at least supposed to be participatory. On the other hand, it can be argued that the circus is heir to the carnival, and thus a form of popular, as opposed to bourgeois and intellectual, culture.

serve *skazka* and its images, to show that the genre might be successfully adapted to serve the Revolution while delighting the imagination of Soviet children.

Olesha has admitted that the images which moved him most deeply in *skazka* were images of magic change and sudden transformation,[17] such as the story of Pinocchio, or that of the ugly duckling who became a swan. Yet, unlike Aleksei Tolstoi's tale about a wooden man,[18] nothing magical actually happens in *The Three Fat Men.* There is, to be sure, a doll of wondrous construction, which does grow, but it remains a doll; it does not become a little girl. It is only a creation of science.

Despite the fact that in *skazka* miracles might well be allowed to happen, Olesha begins his story by appealing to his reader's rationality. He is not going to insult the child's intelligence, he says, with a foolish tale about sorcerers. At each seemingly mysterious happening, Olesha assures the reader that in the end everything will be explained according to the iron laws of logic. Indeed, he makes his hero a scientist.

Gaspar Arneri is the first of Olesha's doctor-heroes. In his own way, like the circus people of *The Three Fat Men*, he is a daring conqueror of man's limitations. Indeed, he is the per-

[17] "Pervoe maia," p. 312. Olesha often uses his favorite *skazka* visions as central images around which to crystalize works which are not themselves *skazka*. *The List of Blessings,* for example, a play about an actress' struggle to reconcile the old and the new within herself, builds on the image of the ugly duckling. Although the actress, Goncharova, claims that there are no ugly ducklings in Soviet society, that everyone is born a swan, there is a part of her that feels that Soviet society really forces everyone to remain an ugly duckling. She dreams of flying away on silver wings, of being freed and transformed. Instead, she is killed during a strike-breaking riot in Paris, a victim of her own internal contradictions.

[18] Tolstoi told Olesha that he wanted to write a tale about a wooden man, a variation on a book which had much impressed him when he was a boy. In Tolstoi's tale, the wooden man would meet up with a puppet theatre, and the puppets would immediately recognize him and call him by name although it would be the first time they had ever seen him. Olesha was enchanted by the idea. ("Vstrechi s Alekseem Tolstym," pp. 398-99.)

fect Oleshan hero: an intellectual whose knowledge brings him power and respect in a world of men of action and athletes.

Nevertheless, Gaspar Arneri always works within the limits of rational possibility. Though he does transform the tightrope-walker Tibul into a black man by means of a potion and later changes him back by means of an antidote. The change is, however, a superficial one—a change of color, not of essence. Tibul is not, for instance, changed into a man of steel or wood. Nor does he suddenly acquire the gift of flight or of immortality. Even in Olesha's *skazka,* then, only the scientifically conceivable changes actually occur. The others are only seeming.

Thus, despite his inordinate longing to free himself from life's limitations through the exercise of his artistic imaginaton, even in *skazka* Olesha keeps within narrow limits. Despite all the wondrous seeming transformations, everyone is ultimately condemned by Olesha to be what he is, not what he would be. His characters can have no more freedom than his own imagination has from the laws which govern it, and Olesha himself is trapped by an imagination whose images are inevitably controlled by the contents of his own memory.

Olesha's memory, the reservoir from which he must draw colors and themes for artistic transformation, is filled with images out of the old culture in which he grew up. He repeatedly tries to explain how he has been crippled since the emotions and memories which he considered his artistic "wealth" were declared by Soviet critics to be "worthless."[19] Artistically, he cannot afford this loss of the relevance of childhood images and sensations. He is committed to childhood as the source of all beauty and fresh perception, but now his own childhood must be regarded as having been a waste: the accumulation of outdated images and symbols, a long and often

19 See: "Rech' na pervom vsesoiuznom s'ezde sovetskikh pisatelei," *Povesti i rasskazy*, pp. 426-28.

unpleasant training in the values of a world which no longer exists.

Olesha's creativity thus becomes doubly dependent on childhood memories: not only as the source of all that is fresh, clean, and poetic in his imagery, or as the memory of a period when responsibility was still in the future, but also as the explanation, almost the excuse, for a feeling of inadequacy to the Soviet present. Olesha declares that he was spoiled, perhaps permanently debilitated by being brought up as the child of bourgeois parents in the period immediately preceding the Revolution. In stories contemporary with "Love" [1929], such as "I Look at the Past" ["Ia smotriu v proshloe," 1928], "Human Material" ["Chelovecheskii material," 1928], "The Chain" ["Tsep'," 1929], as well as in the later "From the Secret Notebooks of Fellow-Traveler Zand" [1932], Olesha describes childhoods filled with resentment.

The events and tone of these stories correspond closely to that of the childhood Olesha later claims for his own in the autobiographical *No Day without a Line*. On occasion, Olesha even closes the early stories with an explicit identification of the child hero with himself.[20] Whether or not the specific incidents ever "happened" exactly as they are described in these stories, or indeed "happened" at all, the stories are clearly intended as part of Olesha's moral autobiography. Together with *No Day*, they present a coherent image of a childhood which Olesha wishes to preserve as his. It is not childhood remembered only as a sunlit paradise, but more often childhood as a trap from which he has been released neither by growing up nor by the Revolution, a trap which continues to imprison his imagination because it occupies the most significant part of his memory.

In several of the stories mentioned above, Olesha insists

[20] See particularly "Tsep'," and "Chelovecheskii material," *Izbr. soch.*, pp. 249-60.

that already as a child, he was oppressed by his family's dreams for him. He was uncomfortable and constrained in the school uniform which symbolized the subordination of his life to other people's plans. He sees himself as if from the outside, as a ridiculous, and above all, pitiful figure: "I have the closely cropped hair of a gymnasium student, my head isn't round, not quite a child's head. The back of my head is cut off flat. [. . .] Perhaps a phrenologist would have diagnosed a love for solitude, bashfulness, easily aroused modesty—everything that for some reason is called 'sickliness' when one speaks about a child."[21]

In "Human Material" he describes his gymnasium uniform which "stood by itself around my body and was taller than it, and [the] shoulders had nothing to do with my shoulders. [It] surrounded me, hard, wide, immobile as a chair back!"[22]

Olesha scorned from the first his father's ambition that he become an engineer, mostly because it was his father's choice for him. He built up a formidable resistance to the whole idea: ". . . in that part of the brain where, in a future engineer, an inclination for draftsmanship is concentrated, I had a blind spot. I sensed the scientific impossibility of setting in motion something which wasn't there at all. This realization transformed itself into a headache, a weight which pressed against the bones of my forehead." (p. 252) He retreats into sickness, an explanation of inadequacy which allows him to feel persecuted and put upon by others. Although his parents gave him a drawing compass to "stimulate his talent," he records his first struggle with it as a lethal combat:

In its velvet case, its legs tightly clamped together, there lies a cold, gleaming compass.

It has a heavy head. I am about to pick it up. It suddenly opens,

[21] Olesha, "Ia smotriu v proshloe," *Izbr. soch.*, p. 289.

[22] "Chelovecheskii material," p. 251.

and its point pricks my hand. I hold one of its legs in my fist. Its movement is much swifter than I had anticipated, even faster than my warning reflexes. I raise my hand to my mouth to lick off the blood—and I don't even have time to think "watch it" . . . the compass has already swung around in my fist and looks into my eyes with terrible sharpness. And I don't understand what is going on: What is it? What is that gleam? What is that point that I cannot grasp physically and which menaces me with death? (p. 252)[23]

Engineering and the tools associated with it, cold, sharp, and terrifying become threats with which others, and especially his father, wish to destroy the boy's vision of himself and his own potential masculinity. Olesha rebelled against all such constraining devices as a uniform, a compass, and predrawn dotted lines to cut along, anything which resembled a trap. Conversely, he remembers with pride his ability to draw straight lines without a ruler. He could create, and make his way without the limiting structures imposed on him by others.

He felt degraded not only by his parents' hopes for him but further by their suspicions that he had nasty habits:

Worse yet, they also suspected that in children's conversations, thoughts and desires there was always something improper. [. . .]

"He probably keeps his hands under the blanket."

They exchanged significant looks, and I saw *that* fear in their glances.

I didn't have that nasty habit. I had no intentions of keeping my hands under the blanket. They imposed that desire on me. I was always under suspicion. They looked at me searchingly and read

[23] *Ibid.*, p. 252. People kept demanding that Olesha become an engineer, that he adopt the very profession which, by its concern for structural problems, was most alien to the workings of his mind. His father, who first wanted him to be an engineer, was superseded by Stalin, who demanded that writers become "engineers of human material." No wonder Ivan Babichev, who declares "I have invented myself," has chosen to invent himself as a former engineer rather than a former anything else!

in me sexual thoughts which were not there. ("Ia smotriu," pp. 285-86)

Olesha refuses any imputation of guilt. Once more he was the innocent, maligned by others. Actually, he did not dislike feeling martyred, and records that he enjoyed feeling insulted, often provoking the feeling in himself because "melancholy and a feeling of offense can be pleasant and cheerful." (p. 290) He attributes even to his boyhood self the possession of that secret which will transform melancholy into cheerfulness: "I can use [the secret] at any moment. But I like being melancholy. I close my eyes, and a sweet shiver runs through me. I open my eyes, and in the midst of the blue sky I see a rainbow because there are tears on my eyelashes." (p. 290) He chooses to be a victim.

The boy transforms his self-induced melancholy by self-dramatization. For example, he sees himself accompanying the hero of a book he was reading: "The hero lives in France. I raise my eyes. There is a brick wall in front of me, and green foliage moves against the brick. This is my France [. . .] France, country of my future . . ." (p. 291) The boy then moves off into one of those daydreams of Western Europe, its culture, its beauties, its personal freedom, from which the man could never completely free himself.

In *No Day without a Line*, Olesha maintains that certain childhood experiences had marked him for life. For instance, he had once been put on a bad-tempered colt. Two ragged boys laughed at him, Olesha says, hoping he would be thrown and killed. Although he managed to slip off to safety, "the boys laughed, and I was ashamed. I was no warrior, not a man but a coward, a dreamer, kindly, an old man, a turd . . . . It was then, at the hour of sunset, in the steppe near Voznesensk that my character was defined forever." (*Ni dnia*, p. 30) Olesha is describing a moment which is really one of choice, wherein he takes up the stance of a persecuted coward, and accepts the world's definition of him. He will not challenge this definition of his physical being, and accepts the vision of himself as already "old," and therefore always condemned to bodily helplessness. Only much later, by making the world see him as he chose to be seen, through his art, could he hope to overcome this first characterization of himself by others.

Olesha's own father appears as the most menacing figure of his childhood. The echoes of "the tragedy" of the father's losses at cards weighed heavily on the whole family, particularly as he continued to frequent "The Club" despite the fact that everyone knew he had no luck. Thinking about these losses, Olesha chooses to picture his father being humiliated: "We knew nothing about Papa's existence at the Club. Perhaps he became covered with perspiration when he lost. Perhaps he told stories to put people he wanted to borrow three rubles from in a good mood. Perhaps people exchanged significant glances with one another while they chatted with him." ("Ia smotriu," p. 285) His father sometimes came home drunk. And once:

> I remember the time that Papa stood me on the window sill and took aim at me with a revolver. He was drunk. Mama implored him to "stop it," and fell on her knees before him. . . [. . .]
>
> So, there I was standing on the sill, and my father was aiming at me. It was, of course, a joke; nevertheless one thing was clear: Papa shouldn't drink. (*Ni dnia,* p. 16)

Olesha's father took him to the barber for haircuts which left him feeling shrunken and violated. Worst of all, his father would introduce him to people by saying, "Meet the heir." Olesha always refused that identification, not only on the grounds that his father had already lost the money that he, the son, should have inherited, but also because the father was the guilty one, and the son the persecuted innocent. In *No Day without a Line,* he wrote his final judgment on his relationship to his father: "A repetition of him? No, I was alone, alone in the world and even now, I am alone." (p. 19)

Olesha mentions this isolation from his father several times. As early as "I Look into the Past" he attributed great significance to it:

> It seems to me that the development of a man's destiny and character is to no small degree predetermined by whether or not the boy was fond of his father.
>
> Perhaps one can divide men's characters into two categories: one is made up of those who were formed under the influence of filial love, the other of those ruled by a thirst for liberation, a secret, unconfessed thirst, which unexpectedly, in a dream, takes on the aspect of a shameful event when they strip a man naked and everyone looks at him.[24]
>
> Thus thoughts of running away, the road, the joy of being insulted, thoughts of war, of a soldier, of amputation are formed. [. . .]
>
> Thus begin the quests for a father, a homeland, a profession, a talisman which may turn out to be fame or power. (p. 291)

As we have seen, Olesha did find in his art a talisman which enabled him to achieve a kind of power, even if he did not feel that it had brought him sufficient fame so that he could go home in triumph and dazzle his parents.

If Olesha hastens to reject the image of his father, he feels a much closer bond with his mother, and declares that he always thought of himself as resembling her. He speaks of his consciousness of this resemblance in a description of his first

[24] It is really not necessary, to stop over each of the many sentences in these passages that could bear Freudian analysis. The general significance of the passages seems clear enough for our purposes so as not to require exhaustive comment. Cf. Kavalerov's dream of being stripped of his blanket.

encounter with mirrors, the first time that he saw *himself* reflected back from the world which was *other*, and no longer simply an extension of himself. Once more, Olesha is concerned about the way other people see and define him and how he can make them see him as he himself does, in this case, in the image of his mother:

[. . .] I noticed a resemblance to my mother, and not to my father. I mentioned this discovery, and they laughed at me. But no matter how many glances I threw at the mirror, each one told me that I was right—Mama's face looked back at me. Out of my boy's face, soiled with unclean thoughts, mother's beautiful face! [. . .] Little by little, others too began to exclaim: "How like his mother." [. . .] The more secret my inner life became, the closer I drew to my first love, the more clearly the resemblance to my mother showed through. The surer I felt that I stood on the enchanted threshold of a somewhat different existence linked with woman, the longer my mother's very nose, lips, and eyes lingered in my face, (*Ni dnia*, p. 17)

In "From the Secret Notebooks of Fellow-Traveler Zand," Olesha made resemblance to one's mother into a symbol of weakness as an artist and of inability to meet a new reality. Zand, tying a necktie his mother had given him, cries: "How can a strong man look like his mother?" and his mother answers by playing music by Chopin "whose tender works came from infantile love for himself and fear for himself." Zand says he wants to break himself of the habit of examining himself "the way a baby in the bath looks at his feet and legs." But his final cry is "I want to be an idiot, Mother! What happiness to be an idiot."[25] Zand's cry expresses his desire to return to a condition of irresponsibility for his own life, a condition of dependency, like childhood. Here, as always in

[25] All quotes from "Koe-chto iz sekretnykh zapisei," p. 16.

Olesha's system of imagery, this need to return to a state of childish irresponsibility is linked to a mother figure.[26]

Even Olesha's mother, however, is sometimes brought under the pall of resentment which hangs over his descriptions of childhood. She is sometimes seen as sharing his father's indifference to the dreams and knowledge the boy cherished most. For this indifference as well as their general ability to shame him, the adults in the family had to be punished. The story "The Chain"[27] is the description of such a vengeance.

In "The Chain" the boy is ashamed of what he says, and ashamed of his desire to ride a bicycle belonging to a student who has come courting his sister. As he rides, he gets an insect in his eye, and falters, losing the bike chain. This is a disaster: "The student had a bike, and I broke it. One could put it even more strongly: the student had a wife and I put out her eye." (p. 257) There is no real way back out of this misfortune. So, characteristically, the boy decides to break the normal laws of cause and effect by pretending he is only dreaming. Because he is at fault, he calls up an aggressive, occasionally recurring dream: "I kill Mama. I stand up. Vera [his sister] covers her face with her hands. Mama becomes all squat, becomes fatter, her neck disappears." (p. 258) As he cannot go home, he decides to run away, and is picked up by Utochkin, the champion bicycle racer, to whom he tells a somewhat garbled version of his story. Utochkin takes the boy home in his automobile:

[26] Sometimes this dependency is recognized as sexually debilitating and degrading. The mother figure takes on the slovenly traits of the widow Prokopovich in *Envy*. It should perhaps be mentioned that Olesha *was* married to Olga Suok (whose surname he gave to the girl heroine of *The Three Fat Men*). She edited his posthumous *Ni dnia bez strochki*, and is still living in Moscow. The marriage does not seem to have been a particularly easy one, however. (My only definite information on this matter is an unpublished letter from Petr Ershov.)

[27] Olesha, "Tsep'," *Izbr. soch.*, pp. 254-60.

Now I'm impudent, haughty, and cruel. Where am I rushing? I am rushing to punish Mama, Papa, Vera, the student. . . . If they all died before my eyes right now, I would exclaim with a laugh, "Look, Utochkin! Ha, Ha Ha! They're dying. . . . We're in the car, we're all greasy. . . . Who said, 'love, obedience, pity?' We don't know, we don't care, we have cylinders, gas, fenders. . . . We are men. Look, here's a great man: Utochkin! The man is driving to punish Papa!" (p. 259)

The disaster is turned into a triumph. All the boy's family are to be punished for his own fault. Now they are humiliated and destroyed by the Avenger, a hero with all the traits Olesha attributes to a real man: control over machinery, athletic prowess, and an immense personal fame.

If Olesha chooses to remember and preserve both aspects of the childhood that we see in his autobiographical stories and his memoirs—both the glorious dreams and the resentments—it is because from his adult point of view, the two were necessarily linked. The glorious dreams had crippled him, and the final crime his father committed against him was to teach him the wrong values:

They told me a lot about justice. [. . .] [After the Revolution,] I found out that only that which helps in the liberation of the oppressed class is just. None of those who taught me how to live told me a word about this justice. I should have found it out for myself, by using my head. But what had they stuffed my head with? A dream about wealth, about making everyone bow down before me.[28]

His mother had told him the rebellious students were criminals: "Even mother, even that beautiful figure—mother—was distorted in that terrible world of lies."[29] Olesha claimed that he had no mentor when he first began to think, once more

28 "Chelovecheskii material," pp. 252-53.

29 "Notes of a Writer," p. 151.

trying to evade adult responsibility by claiming that he was corrupted early. He was, of course, not in perfectly good faith, as he recognized that other poets, such as Bagritskii, overcame equally debilitating childhoods. Nevertheless, he envied the children growing up under Soviet power because "their youth which will shine again in their memories will not have to bend the knee and beg forgiveness of their reason: I was so good when the world was so bad."[30]

The Revolution had despoiled him of his brilliant and fresh childhood memories by forcing him to see the early 1900s as a vicious time. How could he now achieve a Soviet glory by writing with images based on dreams that belonged to a dead past? He tried desperately to catch up. In "The Chain" he apostrophized his boyhood self:

> Look at me, what a little distance I've gone from you—and look: I'm already puffed out, too heavy. . . . You were the same age as the century. Remember? Blériot had flown the Channel? Now I've fallen behind, just look how I've fallen behind. I mince along, a fat man on short little legs. . . . Look how hard it is for me to run, but I run, although I gasp for breath, though my legs fail me, I run after the thundering storm of the century! (p. 260)

Run he did, but he was dragged back by resentment, by a load of memories of failures dating from childhood, by current failures caused by the critics' refusal to accept even the good memories of his childhood as relevant, by his failure to make the world see him as he wished to be seen, and finally, by his failure to find anything to write about except these failures themselves.

[30] *Ibid.*, p. 150.

Chapter V

Olesha the Dramatist

Childhood was only one of several themes from the past which oppressed Olesha at the beginning of the 1930s. Others were the longing for fame of a prerevolutionary kind and for Europe, the struggle with vestiges of the past in oneself, and the fear of the artist's estrangement from his fellow men.[1] Olesha called these "lizard themes." There is no way for a writer to drive such a theme from his imagination: "If the writer Zand busies himself with a new, great theme, with the live joyfulness of a "sunny" theme, despite this, one way or another, that black lizard theme, with its stinking tail or its venomous head, will poke through the new work."[2] Olesha maintained, both in his own name and in that of Fellow-Traveler Zand,[3] that such a theme could only be scotched, not

1 Critics, among them Lev Levin, Gleb Struve, and Kornelii Zelinskii, have dealt at some length with certain of these "lizard themes." See: Lev Levin, *Na znakomye temy,* pp. 86-106; Gleb Struve, "Pisatel' nenuzhnykh tem," *Novyi zhurnal,* XXV, 139-58; and Kornelii Zelinskii, *Kriticheskie pis'ma.*

2 Olesha, Introduction to scenes from "Chernyi chelovek," *30 dnei,* No. 6 (1932), p. 27.

3 Zand even repeats arguments and comments that Olesha has used in his own name. For example, Olesha said in a speech to the All-Union Conference of Dramatists held in January 1932: "And I dream passionately, to the point of howling, to the point of tears, I dream of that strength which an artist of the rising class (which I want to be), must have." ("Rech' na dispute 'Khudozhnik i epokha'," in Olesha, *P'esy,* p. 268.) In the same speech, Olesha says: "I thought that art was greater than life. It embraced my life like the sky. . . ." Zand makes both of these remarks in "Koe-chto iz sekretnykh zapisei poputchika Zanda," published almost simultaneously with Olesha's delivery of his own speech.

killed, unless the artist works it out of his system, managing to incarnate it in a story or—even better—a play.[4]

What more therapeutic way to free oneself from themes of isolation and estrangement than to see them expressed in one's own words by other human beings! The drama is the only form of literature which enables an author to influence the behavior of live people, to manipulate them, to force them to share his dreams. In the theatre the text takes on the stuff of an objective reality. As P. Markov observes in his introduction to a volume of Olesha's plays: "Olesha saw in the theatre the possibility of creating, as it were, another, perfectly concrete world apart."[5] Olesha himself said: "It seems to me that no other kind of creation gives one such great satisfaction in the working of the material, in the pleasant feeling that you are a master."[6]

Although Olesha may have been tempted to act in his own dramas, as Maiakovskii had in his, he would have been doubly vulnerable, doubly exposed, had he done so. Projecting his lizard themes on other people was both less compromising and a more thorough purgation. During rehearsals Olesha as author could discuss his characters' problems impersonally. Played out by someone else, they were no longer his private obsessions, trapped within him.

Furthermore, Olesha was evidently caught up in the inexplicably attractive rehearsal atmosphere. Anyone who has ever prepared a play for performance knows it. Shut off from the outside, the almost empty theatre is the center of existence, the place that counts, where your friends are. Relationships rapidly become intense. Participating in the rehearsals of his

4 See "Rech' na dispute 'Khudozhnik i epokha,'" p. 269.

5 Markov, introductory article to Iurii Olesha, *P'esy*, p. 5.

6 Olesha, in *Sovetskaia literatura na novom etape*, the stenographic report of the first plenum of the Organizing Committee of the Union of Soviet Writers, Oct. 29-Nov. 3, 1932. Olesha's speech is on pages 239-40.

own plays must have served an emotional function for Olesha similar to working in the spartan camaraderie of the *Gudok* office. Olesha might well have echoed Blok's comment to their common director Meierkhol'd: "Believe me, it is important for me to be around your theatre. . . . This is for me a purgative moment, a way out of lyric isolation."[7]

To carry the theme of drama as therapy a little further, it is interesting to note how much more violence there is in Olesha's plays than in his earlier works. In *Envy* there are already some incidents of symbolic violence as characters who want to revenge themselves on a world which doesn't recognize their merit lash out in retaliation. Kavalerov turns to verbal assault. Ivan reminisces about his pleasure when, as a boy, he had ripped the pink satin dress of a little girl who had replaced him as the center of attention at a party. Grown up, Ivan enjoys tearing crabs apart, sacrificing them as though he were a priest. Ivan imagines the destruction of Andrei and his Quarter; Kavalerov dreams that Ophelia kills Ivan. And so on. But we never see any real violence physically perpetrated against any character during the time span of the action of *Envy*. In the plays, however, violence, in the form of both imaginary and real murders and crimes of passion, becomes the all-pervasive theme.

Olesha is fascinated by the dramatic possibilities of murder. In "Notes of a Dramatist" ["Zametki dramaturga"], he observes that people never lose their childish fascination with things having to do with blood and death. Murder is therefore a fundamental theme of the drama. It is difficult to think of a play where at least one of the characters doesn't die. Murder, however, like the acquisition of sudden wealth, another favorite theme of the bourgeois theatre, is not an appropriate

[7] Aleksandr Blok, letter to Vsevolod Meierkhol'd, in the Blok archive, TSGALI, Moscow (998-1-1051); quoted in F. D. Reeve, *Aleksandr Blok: Between Image and Idea,* pp. 238-39.

subject for a Soviet dramatist.[8] Now, reflects Olesha, one can destroy a character logically, not physically. A man does not become a corpse; he becomes a zero.[9]

Nevertheless, Olesha wants corpses. *The Conspiracy of Feelings, The Black Man* [*Chernyi chelovek*], the fragmentary *The Death of Zand* [*Smert' Zanda*], and the unfinished play about a theatre doctor—all pivot around crimes of passion, retributions for real or imagined betrayals. As *The Conspiracy of Feelings* is the dramatic adaptation of *Envy*, it enables us to see both the problems Olesha encountered in shifting forms and the startling darkening of tone.

Kavalerov is now completely isolated. The play is not seen through his eyes and his point of view. The significance of this change is immediately clear in the opening scene. *The Conspiracy of Feelings* begins, as does *Envy*, on a sunny morning in Babichev's apartment. Babichev is still doing setting-up exercises. But instead of Kavalerov's resentful internal monologue there is dialogue, and Kavalerov's contention that Babichev treats him as if he weren't there is immediately shown to be false. Even more damaging is the fact that certain observations made by Kavalerov to himself in the novel cannot be reproduced convincingly within a conventional dramatic form. When Babichev does his exercises, Kavalerov can no longer make his comment about Babichev's velvety groin. Further, Babichev himself formulates certain images which in the novel were under Kavalerov's control. For example:

BABICHEV: *Yesterday I was going downstairs somewhere. And as I went down, I felt, the devil knows what, like my breasts were*

[8] Olesha regrets the loss of these and other bourgeois themes. Behind this whole discussion one can feel the haunting fear of many dramatists that there will be no drama (which is based on conflict), indeed that there can be no art in the future conflictless society.

[9] Olesha, "Zametki dramaturga," *Izbr. soch.*, pp. 402-3.

> *bobbing. Do you understand, Kavalerov, my breasts were bobbing like a woman's. . . .* [10]

The individualization of vision and language which makes the peculiar greatness of the novel is almost completely lost in the dramatic adaptation.

Olesha does attempt to give Kavalerov back some control in one scene where the audience sees Babichev through Kavalerov's dream. (The stage lighting signals quite clearly the passage into and out of the dream sequence.) But as the spectators have previously seen Babichev "for themselves," they understand clearly that Kavalerov is projecting his own hatred and jealousy onto Babichev. Kavalerov may dream that Babichev is a crude brute who tries to rape Valia, but the scene does not affect the audience's conception of Babichev.

The complexity of *Envy* is further eroded in the play by Olesha's development of the destructive, petty philistine [*poshlyi*] aspect of Ivan's "conspiracy of feelings." Ivan is no longer simply in search of a man who has attempted suicide for love. (*Envy*, pp. 87-88) Now he tries to provoke a man into killing his mistress' husband. Ivan fails to work the lover up to the kill, but suddenly there is an off-stage scream. The husband appears; he has just killed his wife.

Similarly, having embraced Kavalerov as a conspirator, Ivan tries to convince him to kill Babichev, with whom Valia is in love.[11] Kavalerov, clutching a razor, goes off to do the deed. But no one takes him seriously:

10 "Zagovor chuvstv," *P'esy*, p. 18.

11 In *The Conspiracy of Feelings* Valia is in love with a more humane Andrei Babichev who stays up all night reading *Othello* in Kavalerov's volume of Shakespeare. Volodia has disappeared. For a more complete discussion of the differences between *Envy* and *The Conspiracy of Feelings*, see William Harkins', "Jurij Oleša's Drama *Zagovor čustv*," in the forthcoming *Festschrift* in honor of George Y. Shevelov.

KAV: *Are you Andrei Petrovich's wife?*
VALIA: *Not yet.*
KAV: *I'm going to cut him open with a razor.*
VALIA: *Who, you? All right then, cut! Andrei Petrovich, Kavalerov has come to slice you up!*
A. P.: *Me? Right now? All right, what do you want me to do? Lie down? Take off my collar?*
SHAPIRO: *Well it looks like the Shakespeare's starting!*
A. P.: *What are you going to kill me with?*
KAV: *A razor.*
A. P.: *Yes indeed, we will slice, Kavalerov* [takes the razor from him and cuts the salami]. *Thus, we cut. Smell the aroma?*

In the end, Kavalerov turns on Ivan and kills *him* with the razor instead of Andrei Babichev.[12] Contemporary critics wondered whether this ritual killing meant that Olesha had finally killed the Ivan in himself. *The Black Man* was to show that he had not.

The unfinished *Black Man* is really one of many sketches for *The Death of Zand.*[13] The hero, the ubiquitous Fellow-Traveler Zand, still oppressed by his lizard themes, is here haunted by a new one: murder. On the one hand, he is thinking of killing

[12] In the text of *Zagovor chuvstv* printed in *P'esy*, the final scene has been changed—purged of its violence. In the *P'esy* text, Kavalerov fails to kill either Andrei, Ivan, or himself, and simply collapses like a doll in a heap. The original version is quoted and commented on by V. Kirpotin in his *Proza, dramaturgiia, i teatr*, pp. 150-51. The original version, a copy of which I have in my possession, is in the State Theatrical Archives in Moscow.

[13] Olesha, "Chernyi chelovek," *30 dnei*, No. 6 (1932), pp. 27-31. Another fragment "Otryvok iz p'esy *Smert' Zanda*," was published in *Literaturnaia gazeta*, Oct. 19, 1930. It is full of themes and figures from other Olesha works: the beggar who sits between two pharmacy doors in "Notes of a Writer" (hero of Olesha's projected but unwritten novel, *The Beggar*), the theme of Abel, the righteous one, from "The Cherry Stone," Kavalerov's theme of the dream in which the dreamer will not be punished because he will wake up, the theme of murder through jealousy, and more.

himself, on the other, he intends to write a play about murder. Zand, by working out his obsession in a play, luxuriates in his thoughts of murder without any of murder's inconveniences.

He is particularly fascinated by men who can kill simply and spontaneously. His own references are all literary.[14] Although he thinks of Raskolnikov,[15] who killed in order to prove his strength, Zand speculates that true strength must lie elsewhere:

They say it is the unusual people, the elect, who are strong. Prophets, generals, geniuses. . . . But it's not true. . . . They are possessed. It's not strength, but obsession, unrest. . . . On the contrary, it's all done from weakness, from fear of death. Strength is something different. It's the ordinary people who are strong. Take him, for example. . . . Just look: he wanted to live with you, so he decided to kill the other man. . . . (p. 31)

[14] He therefore shares in the literariness of his creator. Olesha began his career with a cycle of poems on Pushkin's themes. The title of *The Black Man,* as well as the idea of treating the relationship between genius and murder, would seem to be taken from Pushkin's little drama *Mozart and Salieri.* Olesha's literary references are not merely playful, although play is important to Olesha. The fact that works of authors of the past have become a real part of his own life enables Olesha to expand enormously the realm over which his consciousness has complete control. He uses the works of others as his own raw material. They thereby gain an extra fillip of immortality. Olesha's own hopes of immortality rest on the assumption that his own works will be thus assimilated into the creative bloodstreams of other artists.

[15] There is, of course, a strong Dostoevskian influence on Olesha. Zand and Kavalerov share many of the characteristics and preoccupations of the Underground Man. Gleb Struve has recognized this ("Pisatel' nenuzhynkh tem," p. 142), as has Robert L. Jackson in his *Dostoevsky's Underground Man in Russian Literature.* Professor Jackson's book is particularly interesting in its treatment of other early Soviet writers who were concerned with the same "underground" themes. The discussions of Zamiatin's *We* [*My*] and A. Sobol's "Memoirs of a Freckled Man" ["Memuary vesnushchatogo cheloveka"], and of Leonov and Erenburg, make it clear that *Envy* is not an isolated work in the context of the period. See chapter VII.

As the play opens, Zand has come to interview a simple killer, a man who has tried to murder his wife's first husband: the Black Man of the title. The Black Man, a handwriting analyst, who reads lines of genius and murder in Zand's palm, represents all Zand's temptations: "This man's ideology is a parody of the ideologies of Freud, Spengler, and Bergson [. . .] a caricature of European thought in the era of the decline of Capitalism, a parody of those who write about the doom of progress, about the destruction of man's humanity by machines [. . .]" (p. 27) The play was to show Zand's struggle against the ideology of the Black Man with its diabolical temptations of idealism and elegance. Zand, like the second husband, must try to kill the Black Man.

Olesha failed to finish this play, although he had written enough variant scenes to make several plays. He ruminated about Zand; he wrote discussions for him where Zand argued about Soviet society, Kant, and Lenin. Olesha's problem with Zand's play was more emotional than technical. Zand was the closest to him of all his characters: he gave Zand, verbatim, arguments he himself used to plead his own case at the All-Union Conference of Dramatists held in January 1932.[16] Olesha could not treat Zand like a simple lizard theme, working him out and letting him stand on his own. To put Zand on the stage would have been tantamount to appearing on the stage himself; to exposing himself directly and totally.

Olesha did finish one play about an artist's struggle to overcome the temptations of European elegance and self-indulgence: *The List of Blessings*. Here, he transposed the problems away from himself, making the main character an artist, but of a different kind: not a writer, or actor, but an actress. Goncharova could make explicit the common predicament of artists in the Soviet Union. Her reasoning admits the justice

[16] See note 3 to this chapter.

of the Revolution, but emotionally she cannot accept it. She believes in the privileges of talent, in her right to live and not be sacrificed in the name of some distant future. She feels herself being torn apart, a person from the Old World, fighting with herself:

I can neither flee, nor revolt, nor lie, nor build. I can only understand and be silent. [. . .] The Revolution has deprived me of the past, but it has failed to show me the future. My thoughts became my present. I did nothing but think. [. . .] A human life is natural only when thought and feelings are in harmony. I was deprived of that harmony. [. . .] I understand everything, that's my trouble. Help me. I don't know what is happening to me. I am all alone in the world. There is nothing but me. And the whole struggle of the two worlds rages in my soul. I'm not fighting you, I'm fighting myself. . . .[17]

Goncharova goes abroad, secretly intending never to return. Though by the end of the play she realizes that she cannot live abroad, that she loves the Soviet Union and its "List of Blessings," unfortunately she has compromised herself too seriously to go home again. She blocks a bullet intended for a French communist leader, but her last request, to have her body covered with a red flag, is ignored: the French workers need their flag as they go to battle the police.

Kirpotin indignantly noted that in *The List of Blessings* Olesha had once more reduced the problem of the Revolution

[17] Olesha, *Spisok blagodeianii* (Berlin-Charlottenburg: Izdat. "Kniga i stsena," 1931), pp. 9, 12, 15. There is an interesting parallel in a letter of Dostoevskii, as quoted in Jackson, *The Underground Man in Russian Literature*, p. 29:

"Of course, terrible is the dissonance, terrible the imbalance which society creates in us. External and internal things should be in equilibrium. For, lacking external experiences, those of the inward life gain the upper hand, and that is most dangerous. The nerves and fantasy then take up too much room in one's consciousness. Every external happening from want of habit seems colossal and somehow frightening. We begin to fear life."

to a subjective conflict within an individual rather than seeing it as a conflict between persons who represent classes. Other critics objected to Meierkhol'd's direction, or to the structure of the play itself. Like *The Conspiracy of Feelings,* which has seven scenes, *A List of Blessings* is divided not into acts, but into eight scenes of unequal length. In this somewhat faulty dramatic structure, momentum is lost in the simple linear progression.[18]

In the drama, as in his narrative fiction, Olesha seems much more comfortable in small, concentrated forms where he need not concern himself with the articulation of heavy masses. Aware of this, Olesha proposed in an article published in *30 dnei* to update a form practiced by Pushkin and Blok: the "little drama."[19] His announced intention was not to write psychological or poetic "closet drama" but to create easily performable, short works of immediate contemporary relevance. He would, for example, dramatize a statement of Engels:

> Before the first stone was made into a knife by the human hand, such a long period of time had to pass that in comparison with it, the historical period would seem insignificant. But the decisive step was taken, and the hand became free. . . .
>
> Thus the hand is not only the instrument of work; it is also the product of work. . . .[20]

[18] An expectation of tension, climax, and denouement is built into the standard three, four, or five act dramatic forms but is lacking in the episodic structure of *Spisok blagodeianii.* The director, Meierkhol'd, was very concerned with the need to create dramatic tension in the production. He placed the characters in unexpected areas of the stage, refusing to place them stage center, in order to make the audience feel "off balance." Meierkhol'd also wanted to present the play without a break, so as not to lose accumulated momentum in an intermission. ("Spisok blagodeianii" in *Stat'i, pis'ma, rechi besedy, 1917-54,* pp. 251-52).

[19] Olesha, "O malen'kikh p'esakh," *30 dnei,* No. 8 (1933), pp. 64-65. Reprinted in *P'esy,* pp. 287-91.

[20] *Ibid.,* p. 289.

Though the "little drama" was to be a short form of great pedagogical usefulness, developing socialist themes into simple images, it is somewhat difficult to see exactly how Olesha intended to go about dramatizing the thought of Engels. Perhaps he did not really know himself. It is doubtful that he ever had any such play staged, but a year after his article he did publish a "little drama" in *30 dnei.*

It is a rather peculiar play, certainly nothing any of his critics could have considered a step forward in revolutionary literacy. Once more, as in *The Three Fat Men,* Olesha falls back into political parable, writing a schematized, fairy tale version of so decisive a revolutionary event as the deposition of a tyrant. Once more, he has avoided putting proletarian characters on stage, clothing his hero in a harlequin costume and making him an actor. There are no workers in the play at all, although one does hear the people shouting off stage, beyond the palace wall. The action takes place in an imaginary time, in a never-never city which is disturbingly reminiscent of the setting for Blok's "The King in the Square" ["Korol' na ploshchadi"].

Olesha would certainly have claimed that his "Play on an Execution Block" ["Igra na plaku"] descended from Maiakovskii's *Mystery Bouffe* [*Misterii Bouff*] rather than from Blok.[21] The grotesque figure of the Minister who guffaws at the workers' slogan "Sun for the miners too!" and their proposal to turn the royal meadows over to the poor would be at home among the Clean on Maiakovskii's ark. But Olesha's language has none of the crass vitality of *Mystery Bouffe.* He has chosen to write in conventional alexandrines, with a tight *abab* rhyme scheme, so that his poetry has no dynamic thrust, and the whole play takes on a formalized, genteel, and un-Soviet tone.

Clearly, Olesha's hope that the "little drama" would enable

21 He did say that the "little drama" should be written as if for a doll theatre, the device of Blok's "The Puppet Show" ["Balaganchik"].

him to come to grips with socialist themes in a more immediate way was not realized. The form could not provide the solution to his inability to write something Soviet critics would consider relevant. Olesha was right, however, in thinking that the "little drama" was a form congenial to him. "Play on an Execution Block" is a pretty thing, a controlled musing about the interrelations between "role-playing" in life and in art.

The plot can be summarized briefly. The day after a revolt has been put down and its leader, a general, executed on the block in front of the palace, three actors come to play before the tyrant. They explain that they play without make-up, stage, or script, and involve all members of the audience, willing and unwilling, in their improvisation. The tyrant says that kings always play roles and that he is himself "somewhat of an actor." There is a great deal of play on the word *igrat'*, meaning to act—as in a play—or to play a game. The same ambiguity works for *igrok:* actor, player, gambler, and *igra:* performance, game, play.

As the off-stage tumult of the people grows greater, the king puts aside dealing with it and agrees to "play" with the actors. Ultimately, he "plays" the role of a king who has just been deposed and is about to be executed. At the fatal moment, the king has a real presentiment of death, and the actor who plays a revolutionary hero really chops off the king's head, ending the play—which is at the same time both play and reality—within the play, and the play itself.

The hero, Ganemede,[22] has proved that the artist can both

[22] The name *Ganemede* also crops up in *The Three Fat Men.* There, however, the bearer of the name is no handsome revolutionary hero but the doctor's old housekeeper, Auntie Ganemede. Mythological speculations are therefore probably out of place, and the name is likely to be a private joke. A clear instance of such a private joke is the incident in *The Three Fat Men* where Auntie Ganemede traps a mouse. The source is revealed in Lidia Libedinskaia's memoir *Zelenaia lampa* [*The Green Lamp*], pp. 22-27.

incarnate revolution through his art and also be himself revolution incarnate. Olesha has made a work of art about an artist, who, by being an artist, is also actively a revolutionary, and whose art coincides with revolutionary action. To present this play is to have the action of art embodied and seen as revolutionary by spectators. Thus, acting becomes action. Unfortunately, when the curtain comes down the ambiguity is dissipated. As in Blok's "Puppet Show," when the set or the curtain falls the stage is revealed, and real revolutionaries don't accept plays about revolutionary harlequins as revolutionary acts.

Olesha was once more trapped in his own circle. So long as the subject matter of his works reflected his own conception of the relationship of art to revolutionary action and socialist construction, he was like a wheel which could not mesh with the larger machine. By 1934 Olesha could no longer convince himself that simply finding a new form would enable him to write to please himself and yet make him acceptable to Soviet critics. He could not hide the fact that almost all his recent writing was always about an artist seen by an artist—ultimately about himself.

Chapter VI

A Last Attempt at a New Subject: The Theme of Soviet Youth

We have seen that by 1934 Olesha's apparently whimsical and unfettered imagination was inscribed in an ever narrowing circle of possibility. Given the continued existence of the Soviet Union, several facts are clear. He could not write a new *Envy*, another novel based on the idosyncratic vision of a man whose imagination had been formed in a prerevolutionary culture. Nor does the seemingly more objective form of the drama provide a panacea. Unlike his earlier, fresh handling of the prose narrative, he brought nothing new to the drama. His best plays are adaptations of his own novels, artistically less successful than their originals largely because the leading character has lost control over the point of view.[1] Olesha could not even finish the play most important to him.[2] At bay, he sees himself in the terrible image of the outcast.

The storm of thoughts doesn't break out of the confines of the man's sick skull. He tries to curb the storm, pulling his head down into his shoulders, and only occasionally does he turn back to look

[1] Even *The Three Fat Men* as presented by the Moscow Art Theatre was by Olesha's own admission "heavy." ("Moia rabota s MXAT," *P'esy*, pp. 319-24.)

[2] Olesha's failure to complete "The Death of Zand" is a first manifestation of the inability to "finish" anything he cared about which characterized the rest of his creative life. He pottered about, working over fragments, convincing himself that he was still writing *something*.

at those who laugh at him. And then the laughers see that on the face they always found so amusing, there glares a dog's snarl.[3]

There is a hunted dog in him; there is a lizard self:

> I grab myself in myself. I grab by the throat that "I" who suddenly wants to turn and stretch out his arms to the past.
>
> The "I" who thinks that the distance between us and Europe is only a geographical one.
>
> The "I" who thinks that everything which occurs is only his life, my unique, unrepeatable, all-embracing life, which, when it ends, will also destroy everything that exists outside me.
>
> I want to choke the second "I," the third one, and all the "I's" who creep out of the past. (p. 253)

The shift from the third to first person possessive pronouns makes it clear that the second and third "I"s are really integral parts of his present "I". Olesha must try and stifle his intimate conviction that even if the world does go on without him it would not matter. He is the central phenomenon in the world, and *he* is precisely his consciousness of both his present existence and his past.

One solution would have been to emigrate, and, like Bunin, write moving, sensually evocative reincarnations of the pre-Soviet past from Paris.[4] But this would not have solved Olesha's problem. It is to misunderstand and oversimplify the intensity of his torment not to realize that Olesha loved not Old Mother Russia but the Soviet Union, and precisely its aspects which seemed most dangerous to his vision. He loved the Volodias, the strong, committed Soviet Youth. At the moment when Olesha feels most deeply that he and his vision are worthless, youth comes to his rescue. In the process of imagining a novel to be called *The Beggar*, which would be about

[3] "Ia smotriu," *Izbr. soch.*, p. 291.

[4] Particularly, *Zhizn' Arseneva.*

his spiritual impoverishment, Olesha stumbles onto the possibility of a new imaginative synthesis. In *The Beggar*, he would wander homeless, sleeping in nooks and crannies. One day he would walk through a narrow arch in a wall into incredible greenness. He would cross the sill and discover that he was young again: "Suddenly, for some unknown reason, youth has returned. I see the young skin of my hands, I'm wearing a soccer jersey, I have become young—I'm sixteen years old. Nothing is inexorable; all doubts and torments have gone. I have become young. Life is all before me."[5] (This passage back into youth is an obvious variation on Wells' image of the door in the wall.)

Once he had experienced the vision of returning youth, Olesha was freed from the beggar theme, because he realized that the solution for him lay in turning to young Communists and writing about them, reliving his own youth in their youth. As Olesha explained to the First All Union Congress of Soviet Writers:

> There was much in my youth, my dreams, my relations with the world, which even now I can depict in a work as the attribute of the man of the new world, of the young Komsomol or worker. The world has gotten younger. [. . .] I have matured, my thought is firmer, but the colors within me have remained the same. Thus the miracle I dreamed of while looking through the arch has actually taken place. Thus youth has returned to me. [. . .]
>
> I want to create a typical young man, making him out of the best there was in my youth. [. . .]
>
> I myself have set myself the task of writing about the young. I shall write plays and stories in which the characters will solve moral problems. Somewhere, there lives in me the conviction that Communism is not only an economic system but also a moral system, and the first to embody this aspect of Communism will be our young men and women.

5 "Rech'," *Povesti i rasskazy*, p. 427.

> I shall put into these works all my sense of beauty, of gracefulness, of nobility, my whole vision of the world [...] so as to show that the new Socialist attitude towards the world is a human attitude in the purest sense of the word. Such is the resurrection of my youth. I did not become a beggar.[6]

Since Olesha could no longer write out of his own experience alone, looking for all his other characters within himself, he would do the next best thing: seek himself in others. It is a last chance.

In a sense, Olesha's new subject was only the logical development of his long standing respect for the more athletic kind of male beauty, which he now equated with adequacy in the new world. It is, for example, because Maiakovskii combined poetic genius with this kind of physical adequacy in his hulking body that Olesha worshipped him. When Olesha knew him, Maiakovskii was handsome, committed to the Revolution, if often at odds with it, and the possessor of a legendary fame during his own lifetime. Olesha was ten years younger, and his admiration for Maiakovskii was almost feminine in its fervor:[7] "I was in love with Maiakovskii. When he arrived, I was overcome with confusion, I trembled when, for some reason or other, he turned his attention to me. . . . As for *my* attention, it was on him all the time, I didn't miss one gesture, one

[6] *Ibid.*, pp. 429-30.

[7] A revealing sidelight on this relationship is cast by the fragment in *No Day* where Olesha compares his attitude toward a bullfight film with that of Maiakovskii: "I was both a woman in love with the matador, and, on the contrary, I particularly despised women at that moment. And all the time, my heart was pounding, and I was ready to shout together with the whole ancient arena. Maiakovskii would have had an answer for me. When he saw a bullfight, he was sorry that there wasn't a machine gun mounted in the bull's horns to mow down the spectators." (pp. 176-77) Maiakovskii identified with the tormented, violent animal. Olesha does not see himself in combat, but helpless and in love with the fearless, handsome matador.

glance, not even a single word." (*Ni dnia,* p. 150) He was under the spell of Maiakovskii's amazing eyes:

> He had incomparable eyes, large and black, and a gaze which, when we met him, made it seem that it was the only thing in the world at that moment. It seemed as though there was nothing around us. Only that glance existed.
>
> When I think of Maiakovskii, I immediately see those eyes [...] They look at me, and it seems to me that the world has become quiet, secret. What kind of a gaze was it? The gaze of genius. (*Ni dnia,* p. 152)

Once Olesha met Maiakovskii at a reception for George Bernard Shaw: "[. . .] the whites of his eyes and the black circles of the irises were visible in the dimness of the corridor—and I felt both pleasure and dread." (*Ni dnia,* p. 237)

Maiakovskii's genius accounted for much of his charisma, but Olesha could also be moved by much simpler men of the same physical adequacy, men such as the sailors who played an important role in the Revolution. In *No Day without a Line,* Olesha recalls that when he was a boy one of the adults he most wanted to resemble was a sailor, Richard Gross. "The collar of his white sailor's blouse lay attractively on his shoulders, and his white neck rose out of it like a beautiful pillar" (p. 41) He commemorates the handsome sailor Anatol Zheleznikov, a reader of Maeterlinck's *Bluebird,* who died, pistols blazing, on the Don. (p. 131)

Olesha needed to feel comradeship with such men. He claims that nothing, not even being called "maestro," gave him more pleasure than being called *bratishka* (an affectionate diminutive of the word meaning "brother") by sailors in blockaded Odessa. (pp. 251-52) He remembers being in a streetcar with a Red Army commander:

> When in the presence of a commander, one has a peculiar, complicated feeling. [...] I thought he was much the better man.

Somehow better, I don't know how. He carried ice skates. He held terrible cold with a glint in his hands. Very keenly, so there was a rasping feeling in my throat, the greatness of the Soviet idea became clear to me. I looked at this clear-eyed young face and thought: there is the last soldier on earth.[8]

In this physical respect for the military man, the man of violence, there is something of the same ambivalence as in Babel's feelings for the Cossacks with whom he served. As Olesha himself comes to feel more and more left behind by these men, they appear even more frequently in his works, less now objects of emulation than of an admiration akin to longing.

Olesha says he admired his friend, the ailing poet Bagritskii, because of his ability to identify himself and his art with such men: "He was in love with warriors." After quoting lines from Bagritskii's "The Last Night" ["Posledniaia noch' "], Olesha concludes:

> I can think of no more sublime lines devoted to a man, a soldier, than these lines written by a poet [. . .] condemned by illness to childlike helplessness.[9] [. . .]
>
> Perhaps Bagritskii is the most perfect example of how an intellectual arrives at Communism by his own paths. (381)
>
> Bagritskii was the poet of joyful Bolshevism, which is why the country built his tomb so high. (p. 383)

In *No Day* Olesha expressed the probably sincere conviction that it is not enough for a really great poet to be "only a poet; Dante, Pushkin, Byron and Maiakovskii, all participated in

[8] "Notes of a Writer," p. 150. Olesha found these young officers very handsome. Sometimes there is "a sort of naïve importance in their carriage and the expression of their faces. Then they look like young scientists." (p. 149) Once again, he underlines the connection which exists in his mind between physical prowess and the mastery of technology.

[9] "Eduard Bagritskii," p. 380.

the great struggles of their times." (p. 143) Even Bagritskii had no need to feel ashamed, as he had served. But Olesha had participated only minimally in the Revolution. He was, of course, only fifteen in 1914, but in 1917 he was eighteen. By the time he was only thirty-one, however, Olesha had already begun to express his feeling of distance from military men as one of being much older than they. Once more, we notice the curious phenomenon that Olesha feels that he had always been either too young or too old, never an adult in full command of his powers:

> I am very old. [. . .]
>
> A few days ago, I was sitting in a trolley opposite a policeman. He had a moustache, the large blond moustache of "the Nordic *bogatyr*." [. . .] And suddenly I realized that the policeman was younger than I. A tall man, a family man, with well-developed chest and shoulders, wearing sweat-soaked boots, and younger than I!
>
> Meanwhile, despite the fact that I'm thirty-one and already notice on myself and in myself signs of physical aging, nonetheless, I have never yet felt as though I were an adult.[10]

Indeed, almost all the characters with whom Olesha identifies his own views and sensibilities are either prematurely aged (Kavalerov feels "cooked" at 27) or actually past their prime: Bohemskii, the old intellectual in "Al'debaran" who loses out in the struggle for Katia's love to the blandishments of youth and to the planetarium where she and her boyfriend can see the stars even when it's raining; the old scientist in "Natasha," who loses his daughter to Stein the parachutist; and the various theatre doctors, all in love with much younger women. Their failure in love is in a sense justified by their age.

Conversely, the "new people" are all young, if not chrono-

[10] "V mire," p. 339.

logically then metaphorically. In *The Conspiracy of Feelings*, Ivan explains this to Kavalerov:

KAV.: *I'll take Valia away from him.*
IVAN: *Oh no,* [. . .] *your youth has gone, Kavalerov.*
KAV.: *That's not true. I'm twenty-eight. He's older than I, and still she loves him.*
IVAN: *You're a thousand years old, Kavalerov. Don't giggle, Anna Mikhailovna, your Kolia is old, he's ancient. He has all the scleroses of the century in him. . . . But my brother, my brother is young.* (p. 63)

The New Men have all the attributes of youth. They are proud in the consciousness of their physical and moral strength, and in their ability to control nature. They are the masters of technology. In Grisha, the hero of Olesha's movie scenario *A Strict Youth*, all these qualities are combined: "Clear eyes, blond hair, a lean face, a triangular torso, a muscular chest—this is the model of modern male beauty. It is the beauty of the Red Army men [. . .] It comes from frequent association with water, machines, and athletic equipment."[11]

Olesha's admiration for the young Soviet man is not merely physical. It goes along with that romantic, magic vision of technology which marked not only his childhood but also his mature life. Blériot and Lilienthal are joined by Soviet pilots. Describing his own first flight in a 1936 story, Olesha concludes:

I will never forget any detail of that flight. They were all marvelous things; It was a stern, efficient, virile world. [. . .] A man who has just completed a long flight begins to respect himself. He experiences a feeling of triumph. [. . .] If I, merely flying as a passenger on a well-traced route which threatened no danger, nevertheless joined in the feeling of triumph, how strongly must the pilots who open up new air routes across the wild expanses

[11] Olesha, "Strogii iunosha," *Izbrannoe*, p. 211.

of the world feel it. [. . .] Imagine what thrilling emotion must fill a pilot when he returns after a historic flight, knowing that all Moscow is awaiting him.[12]

Thousands of young people aspire to follow in the footsteps of these pilots.

To aspire, says Olesha, means to be confident of one's capacities. Olesha envies this confidence in the new Soviet generation, though at the same time sometimes feeling it insufferable. His story "In Summer" ["Letom"] expresses this ambivalence.[13] A young Communist is looking at the stars through a pair of binoculars. Olesha dislikes him at first glance because he feels that using binoculars to look at the stars is ostentatious.[14] Olesha knows the young man is a proletarian writer, and feels sure that he must be utterly devoid of poetry or artistic imagination.

The young man turns out to be a former railroad worker who had read *Gudok*. He is a self-taught writer, and now is studying the stars, using the binoculars for a real purpose. The young man points out various stars to Olesha, among them Vega. Olesha had often thought about the beauty of the name "Vega," knowing it belonged to a star, but never knowing to which one. Now he sees how well the poetic sound of the disembodied name goes with the distant, beautiful blue star. Olesha says "Vega, Capella, Arktur," discovering that the words make a line of verse. The young man does not understand, but Olesha explains that the names spoken in that order form a dactylic line. The young man is overjoyed by the discovery. Each has taught the other something and they settle

[12] Olesha, "Polet," *Izbr. soch.*, pp. 307-8.

[13] Olesha, "Letom," *Izbr. soch.*, pp. 308-11.

[14] It is the highest kind of poetry to see *as if* one were looking through binoculars: i.e., to imagine one is looking through them. Actually using them as a tool for a real purpose is vulgar. Once more, Olesha betrays his preference for an imagined sensation over a real one.

down together to wait for Capella to rise. The unexpected comradeship is sealed with physical contact, a rare occurrence in Olesha's writings. They are awaiting the appearance of Capella: "Suddenly he stopped. I could sense that he was groping for my hand [. . .] I held it out to him, and he led me forward. In silence and light, the star shone over the sleeping world—greenish, full, fresh, almost moist. (p. 310)

Olesha thanks the young man, and is astounded by the young man's thanking him in return.

> As if it were his sky! As if he were responsible for the whole spectacle! [. . .]
>
> He was the master of earth and sky.
>
> I thought about all the people who had been interested in the stars before me, astronomers, navigators, the discoverers of lands and stars.
>
> "Thanks for your interest!"
>
> The young man had received these lands and stars as a legacy. He had received knowledge as a legacy. (p. 311)

Olesha's tone holds just a shade of resentment at what he considers the presumption of the young man, who is, after all, only a student of the discoveries of others. But the legacy *is* his, not Olesha's. Olesha had been content to look upon the sky as fireworks, as entertainment. The young man tries to know the sky and thus possesses it. He may perhaps discover something himself, as did Kepler, who considered himself the first observer of the sky. Olesha wrote in 1956: "Indeed, if Kepler was the first man to understand the plan, the mechanism, the conflict of the spectacle, then he really was the first observer. The others had looked without comprehension."[15]

Twenty years later, the young man surely did not miss the first sputnik as it passed over Moscow, but Olesha did, because

[15] Notes for *Ni dnia* in *Izbr. soch.*, p. 481.

he looked at a fixed point in the Northwest instead of at the whole quadrant. Olesha exclaims:

I don't quite understand how a sphere the size of those globes on pedestals in gardens could be visible and bright at a distance of a thousand kilometers. But there's no point my trying to understand anything about it.

Why did it happen that I was born not in the era when America was discovered, but in the time when the first man-made satellite appeared? (*Ni dnia*, p. 293)

Similarly, Olesha's mind boggles at the idea of a cyclotron: "He described a machine which produces some kind of essential acceleration of something or other for some reason or other. This apparatus is called a cyclotron. But I want to talk about a cyclodrome!"[16] Olesha maintains this posture of incomprehension throughout his artistic career. He must refuse to understand because comprehension of function would be destructive of his preferred vision of the world. As it is, he is able to hold on to his own wonder at even the simpler products of modern technology: the phonograph record, the electric light, the frighteningly deep Moscow subway escalator.

Although this incomprehension is a necessary literary pose, it is not only that. Technology does remain beyond rational explanation for Olesha. Other men have conquered nature by a knowledge which remains occult for him. Consequently, he is irresistibly drawn to those who exercise some technical competence. They thereby become "charming" [*obaiatel'nye*] almost in the etymological sense of the word: they cast a spell.

Indeed, Olesha admires the Soviet young men as much in their role as the heroes of a certain romance of technology as

16 "Ni dnia bez stroki [*sic*]," *Oktiabr'*, No. 7 (1961), p. 161. Olesha continues: "May they forgive my presumptuous intervention in this world of mind and clarity, of the sign which lights up 'No Admittance,' or 'You May Enter.' So, is a nuclear explosion in short an electrical explosion?"

for their military heroism. For example, he watches a young man fix an overhead trolley wire:

> They had cordoned off the area. The trolleys were stopped. The crowd was silent. [. . .] A young man in rubber gloves climbed up, above the crowd—he was doing something with the wire. He was all attention. And without knowing it—rather, without having time to think about it—he performed before the multitude of spectators. Everyone watched him with rapture, fondly, feeling somehow grateful to him and at the same time envious, wishing to be he, feeling pride in him. That is, they experienced the emotions which arise when one is in love.[17]

In such an intrinsically dramatic situation, says Olesha, life may become art without the intervention of the artist. But this transformation may occur even in less dramatic circumstances. For when he is performing certain kinds of rhythmic physical work, where every movement is essential and useful, a man may become "charming" even if otherwise he has no particular gift for making himself attractive to others.

Such statements raise once again the question of what art is for Olesha if, as he says, life may become art without the intervention of the artist. Is art simply the performance of an action which holds the attention of a fascinated public? Merely the equivalent of an action in daily life and therefore the artist's substitute for an ability to act in the world? Perhaps more than this, but certainly also this.

That is why, in his later works, when Olesha wishes to write about an intellectual who should not be exclusively identified with him, he turns once again to the doctor as hero. The doctor too exercises the charm of occult knowledge:

> A doctor arriving at an accident exerts the fascination of a great wizard. This fearsome man, taking shining steel from his bag, this

[17] "Zametki dramaturga," p. 405.

possessor of a momentary but superhuman grandeur, taking the pulse of the person lying on the sidewalk, summoning stretcher bearers by a movement of his finger, and saying nothing to the crowd about the chances of the victim, this man considers himself the embodiment of what is bombastically called Life and Death.[18]

A great surgeon is always an attractive image. He is a worthy rival to the beautiful young man who is the embodiment of health and power. For the doctor has the power to restore health, to control life and death.[19] In *A Strict Youth*, Grisha's rival, Dr. Stepanov, actually resurrects a girl whose heart had stopped beating. The wonder-working surgeon is both an ultimate image of intellectual fame and an extension of Olesha's healer image: the man who dreams he is a prophet and can perform miracles. Dr. Stepanov, then, is only the last incarnation of Olesha's constant ambition to conquer the limitations of nature.

In fact, according to Viktor Shklovskii the image of the doctor directly continues the traditional image of the acrobat as breaker of natural laws. He says in *Theory of Prose* [*O teorii prozy*] that if writers like Rabelais used the figure of the acrobat to incarnate the image of almost miraculous help, the equivalent role in the modern novel is that of the scientist or doctor.[20]

It is fitting, therefore, that the period of Olesha's major productivity should be bounded by Doctor Arneri and the circus athletes of *The Three Fat Men* (written before *Envy*, although published after it), and Doctor Stepanov and the Komsomol athletes of *A Strict Youth*. The theme of the intellectual hero whose knowledge is needed by the beautiful ath-

18 *Ibid.*, p. 406.

19 Not surprisingly, Olesha was very much struck by the rivalry in Thomas Mann's *The Magic Mountain*, where Hans Kastorp is jealous of the doctor, an all-powerful rival who has the right to see X-rays of the girl they both love. (Notes for *Ni dnia* in *Izbr. soch.*, p. 485.)

20 Viktor Shklovskii, *O teorii prozy*, p. 47.

letes has remained. By the time he wrote *A Strict Youth,* however, Olesha was uncomfortably aware that the doctor and the athlete did not automatically consider themselves interdependent allies in a revolutionary struggle. In this scenario, Olesha's major venture in his new subject of Soviet youth, he tries to confront and then reconcile the representatives of both kinds of "charm," intellectual and physical. They are Dr. Stepanov and Grisha, the handsome Komsomol, of course an engineering student, whom we see once fixing an overhead wire in exact analogy to the young man described above.

There is a love intrigue in the scenario which remains unresolved (Grisha loves Stepanov's young wife), but the central problems of emulation and the privilege of talent are neatly settled. Among the spiritual qualities that Grisha believes a Komsomol should cultivate are not only modesty, truthfulness, and generosity, but also sentiment—the capacity to love waltzes as well as marches. Grisha believes that these qualities are not intrinsically bourgeois, but human qualities which had been corrupted by the power of money. He believes that the power of genius, and reverence for genius—such as the doctor's—will remain in the classless society.

Dr. Stepanov himself is a rather unpleasant, haughty, definitely bourgeois personage. A wealthy professional with no active relation to the Revolution, he is won over by the young Communists when he understands that he has misjudged them. He is astounded to find out that Marx too realized that man will still have both joy and sorrow in a classless society,[21] that

21 Olesha's view that the capacity for suffering is a fundamental human quality, independent of unjust social conditions, is similar to Leonov's in his *Road to Ocean (Doroga na okean).* Ocean is the land of the future, where "man's natural estate had at last been attained—he was free, rejoiced in the work of his hand and brain, and was not exploited. But although they had everything, we often saw people with careworn faces. We understood that they knew sadness, and tragedy too, although it was of a kind more worthy of man's dignity." (p. 425)

unrequited love, that "most magical combination of joy and sorrow," will of course still exist. The girl whom he has just saved reads the doctor part of a manifesto written by Grisha which says: "There is not and cannot be equality. The very concept of emulation destroys the concept of equality. Equality is static; emulation is movement. . . . The first rule is that one must emulate one's betters. [. . .] They are those who design machines, struggle with nature, compose music, formulate thoughts." (p. 244) The doctor is ashamed of his previous attitude, and goes to apologize to Grisha, saying that it is Grisha who deserves to be emulated. Thus, Stepanov should be emulated by youth for the excellence of his knowledge and ability to save, and he must emulate them in their understanding of the meaning of Socialism. This is Olesha's version of a two-way Stakhanovite emulation.

Unfortunately, Olesha's Grisha, a waltz-loving young Communist in a humanist tradition, a builder of Socialism, himself a harmonious human being, clean of body and spirit, was met with derision rather than emulation. *A Strict Youth* was filmed according to Olesha's scenario, and completed in 1936. It was never shown. Jelagin states in his *Taming of the Arts* that the remarkably Aryan physical appearance of the leading man, Dmitrii Dorliak was one of the reasons for the interdiction.[22] The film was officially condemned because the discussion of equality and leveling was considered pretentious, abstract, and empty. The idea that in the future classless society the intelligentsia would be in control was condemned as proceeding from bourgeois technocracy. The "musings" of the producers to the effect that suffering and fear of death are a permanent aspect of man's nature were denounced as "philosophical pessimism directed against the Communist ideals of the revolutionary proletariat." Finally, the producers were charged with

22 Juri Jelagin, *Taming of the Arts*, p. 141.

deviation from Socialist Realism in their use of "formalistic devices and insipid stylization."[23]

Olesha's last hope had failed him. He could not find his own youth again in Soviet youth. In the conditions that prevailed in 1936, even his *A Strict Youth,* a reverent offering on the altar of the New Soviet Man, was judged, like the offering of Cain, unacceptable.

23 Babitsky and Rimberg, *The Soviet Film Industry,* pp. 154-55.

Chapter VII

Olesha as a Writer of the 1920s

Olesha produced little of any artistic interest between 1936 and the publication of parts of *No Day without a Line* in 1956. We can take advantage of this twenty-year hiatus in Olesha's creativity to pause and situate his early works more firmly in their context. Obviously Olesha did not write in isolation. In the 1920s many prose writers developed similar themes, techniques, and devices. Having explored Olesha's imagination, it is interesting to consider several of his contemporaries whose visions had much in common with his, so as to distinguish their common assumptions from the imaginative structures which were peculiarly Olesha's.

Perhaps the essential thing to note about the Soviet 1920s is that the literary context was still very broad. Not only was there a great variety of literary trends and a high-spirited experimentalism within Russia itself, but the frontiers which separated Russia from Western Europe were still permeable. Russian literature could still participate in that extraordinary flowering of experimental art which began before World War I in Russia as well as in France, Germany, Italy, and England.[1]

[1] The flow was not always from west to east. *Variétés*, a Belgian magazine in which all the French Surrealists published, put out a special number, No. 11 (March 15, 1930), devoted to avant-garde Soviet writing. The number included selections from Babel, Shklovskii, Pasternak, Maiakovskii, and Pil'niak, as well as the first chapter of *Envy*.

German Expressionism was very fashionable in Moscow in the 1920s. Although in the heat of the fray Olesha felt obliged to deny that there was anything "expressionistic" about *Envy*,[2] some years later, in *No Day without a Line*, he obliquely admits this influence on his early works:

> In the years immediately following the Versailles peace, there appeared several wonderful German novels. They were called Expressionist. Their authors were Werfel, Perutz, and Meyrink. These novels might well be called fantastic. But their fantasy was not a fantasy sharply divorced from daily life like Hoffmann's. In this Expressionist fantasy, there was a real city, and there were real people, but something strange had happened which had forced real people into terrible positions. It was, if you will, very close to Dostoevskii. [. . .] It was a fantasy born of the wavering of light and shadows, of the obstacles, corners, turnings and stairways along one's route. . . .
>
> It would have been rather hard not to surrender to the enchantment of these writers, particularly for someone who was just a beginner. (pp. 234-45)

Olesha in *Envy* does share the Expressionist taste for combination of humor with terror, for the incongruous. He also plays with the traditional grotesque theme of the confrontation of doubles. But in Olesha, the existence of a double implies a kind of spiritual procreation, not an anguishing division of the self. Furthermore, the careful limitation of his imagination, which we have discussed in previous chapters, keeps Olesha from the nightmare terrors of vermin and madness. Perhaps an even more important difference is that German horror literature of the 1920s aims at demolishing the intellectual structure of a prevailing middle-class view. Olesha, writing in the Soviet Union, transforms the technique into a conservative weapon. This difference undoubtedly explains why contem-

[2] "V mire," p. 345.

porary Soviet critics were almost unanimous[3] in labeling Olesha not a German, but a Frenchman.

Berkovskii called him the "best Frenchman among the Russians," and accused him of sharing the belief of such "impressionists" as Rodenbach, Proust, and Giraudoux that the universe exists only in terms of the perceiving "I."[4] El'sberg and Levin also thought that Olesha was influenced by the early works of Giraudoux,[5] particularly by *L'Ecole des indifférents.* Levin did not confine his discussion to the "picturesque mechanics" of the two authors, but insisted that Olesha had even adopted Giraudoux's fundamental attitude toward reality, seeing it only as "the object of refined contemplation."[6]

Much of what Soviet critics had to say about Giraudoux would certainly have applied equally well to *Envy*. B. Pesis stated that one of the central figures in contemporary French literature was "the indifferent observer, understanding much but [indulging in] a passive, sterile, holiday game of observations."[7] Both Kavalerov and Jacques l'Egoiste stroll without responsibility through a festive world of images. Giraudoux "describes as though he were seeing for the first time [. . .] uses themes as a pretext for improvisation, playing with words and thoughts with the facility of an experienced artist. [. . .]" He creates heroes who "constantly give themselves up to reminiscences of the past and childhood [. . .] suffering a complete lack of will to action."[8] So does Olesha.

3 Polonskii in "Ocherki sovremennoi literatury," p. 192, does say that Olesha is closest to Expressionism.

4 Berkovskii, "O prozaikakh," p. 151.

5 Zh. El'sberg, "*Zavist'* Oleshi," *Krizis poputchikov,* pp. 92-98; Levin, *Na znakomye temy,* pp. 113-14.

6 Levin, p. 114.

7 B. Pesis, "Pisatel'skie nastroeniia sovremennoi Frantsii," *Pechat' i revoliutsiia,* No. 4 (1927), p. 17.

8 A. Frid, review of *L'Ecole des indifférents* in *Pechat' i revoliutsiia,* No. 1 (1928), pp. 195-96.

Olesha himself denied that he was in any way influenced by Giraudoux.[9] Perhaps he was not. But a striking parallel of vision does exist between *Envy* and *L'Ecole des indifférents.* In both works, renovation of perception depends on a non-functional view of the world, a preference for seeing things in terms of their surface rather than their structural form. Jacques l'Egoiste describes himself as follows:

Je n'ai point tant de curiosité, ni d'ambition: Je trouve assez d'épaisseur à la surface du monde. Pour moi, chaque être, chaque chose s'appuie plus fortement sur sa couleur que sur son squelette. De grands ressemblances balafrent le monde et marquent ici et là leur lumière. Elles approchent, elles assortissent ce qui est petit et ce qui est immense. D'elles seules peut naître toute nostalgie, tout esprit, toute émotion. Poète? Je dois l'être: Elles seules me frappent.[10]

Olesha was not the only Russian writing novels in which the narrator strolled idly through the world, without responsibility, amusing himself by observing activity in which he had no real part. Shklovskii, Nabokov, and Erenburg were writing such novels too. There are striking resemblances of tone, general narrative structure, even of detail, between some of their works and Olesha's. But they were in exile, clustered in Berlin. Olesha, in the Soviet Union, felt and wrote as did those young Russian writers who actually were uprooted and cut off from active participation in what was occurring in their homeland.

Shklovskii's *Zoo: Letters not about Love, or the Third Heloise*

9 "Talks with His Readers," p. 81.

10 Jean Giraudoux, *L'Ecole des indifférents,* p. 69. Giraudoux also likes to concentrate light—particularly in the eyes of his characters: "ses prunelles taillent la lumière comme des saphirs étoilés." (p. 17) "Ses yeux [. . .] ramassent le soleil et me l'envoient malicieusement et tendrement comme un enfant qui joue avec un miroir." (p. 20) "Sur les bancs de bois, voici les Russes, dont les yeux inclinés ne peuvent retenir la lumière et n'étincellent que par accident." (p. 63)

[*Zoo: pis'ma ne o liubvi ili tret'ia Eloiza*][11] was in many ways a model for Olesha.[12] Intensely, self-consciously literary, *Zoo* is an epistolary novel. It is made up of love letters to Alia from the writer, who, at the same time, uses the letters to make a novel dedicated to his love.

Shklovskii's letter structure is in response to a need for articulation, understood both as a way to express sentiments to which Alia won't listen, and also as the means of articulating love and lyricism with such descriptive elements as Berlin in the 1920s and brief portraits of other artists. The series of letters provides a frame, and the gaps at the joints are crossed by metaphor: "Obedient to the will of my material, I have linked these elements by means of comparisons; all the descriptions turn out to be metaphors of love."[13]

Shklovskii occasionally even realizes his metaphors: there is a dialogue between a spring flood of true love, which has mounted the steps to Alia's apartment, and a protective, solicitous pair of Alia's slippers. This self-mocking dialogue is almost Maiakovskian, but Shklovskii's metaphorical pain is never so outrageously enormous as that of Maiakovskii, a bear, borne on the flood of his own tears. Shklovskii is just a short-tailed monkey, a member of the Grand Order of Monkeys,[14] caged in the zoo which is emigré Berlin.

The zoo, that eternal rendezvous of the dispossessed,[15] is

11 The alternate title: *The Third Heloise* [*Tret'ia Eloiza*] is an anagram of the name of Elsa Triolet, to whom *Zoo* is dedicated.

12 The self-deprecating humor of tone is particularly close to "The Cherry Stone." Fedia's letters to Natasha, his creation of a book as a monument to the fact that she did not love him, the vision of the rejected lover as a soldier standing guard, also parallel *Zoo*. Shklovskii's fauna make his invisible land more fun than Olesha's, however. The short-tailed monkey is more lively than the stately sisters Imagination and Observation.

13 *Zoo*, p. 9.

14 The king of the Order, Aleksei Remizov, was also in Berlin.

15 One thinks not only of Olesha's trips to the zoo, but also of the sad rendezvous of Katia and Serezha in Tertz's *The Trial Begins* [*Sud idet*].

Shklovskii's central metaphor.[16] The writer himself, bored, in exile, becomes the maker of other zoos:

We, free monkeys, find it hard to walk along the sidewalks, living a foreign life. [. . .] We wander like idiots across the world, in order to be free. We transform everyday life into anecdotes.

We construct little, personal worlds between the world and ourselves: menageries.

We want freedom. (p. 29)

But artistic freedom is not something asured by exile: "I will not exchange my profession of writer, my free passage over the roofs, for a European suit, polished shoes, hard currency, not even for Alia." (p. 30) His artist's liberty is menaced by the Berlin zoo. He is separated from himself, from his country, as he is separated from his beloved—even when she does listen to him. Dialogue with her is talking to someone Europeanized, a member of another civilization, despite her Russian birth.[17] Thus, his last letter is not addressed to Alia. It is a request to the Executive Central Committee of Russia to be allowed to return:

I cannot live in Berlin.

My way of life, my habits, all tie me to today's Russia. I can only work for her.

It is not right for me to live in Berlin.

The Revolution has transformed me. Without it, I cannot breathe. Here, one can only suffocate. (p. 105)

The letter is not unambiguous; it ends with the fear that Russia will mercilessly destroy the prodigal son as though he

[16] Shklovskii even dares to juxtapose to his own prose Khlebnikov's "Menagerie" ["Zverinets"] as an epigraph. This is the poem in which appear the animal images Olesha so much admired.

[17] In letter 19 (which Shklovskii forbids us to read, the type barred by red lines), Alia speaks of her nurse Stesha. Shklovski says that anyone who speaks of her nurse in that fashion is obviously deep-down a Russian. Nevertheless, Elsa Triolet, the third Heloise, did remain abroad.

were a surrendered Turk. But at least it holds out a possibility of living and working. In Berlin, the short-tailed monkey's freedom was a cage.

So Shklovskii returned. Nabokov, whose early novel *The Eye* [*Sogliadatai*] is also set in emigré Berlin, stayed abroad. That Nabokov could continue to function in exile was thanks to his extreme pleasure in making patterns, in setting up total games. The anguish of a Smurov, the protagonist in search of his identity in *The Eye*, had already been subsumed for Nabokov in a satisfying structure:

> The theme of *The Eye* is the pursuit of an investigation which leads the protagonist through a hell of mirrors and ends in the merging of twin images. I do not know whether the keen pleasure I derived thirty-five years ago from adjusting in a certain mysterious pattern the various phases of the narrator's quest will be shared by modern readers, but in any case, the stress is not on the mystery but on the pattern.[18]

Even the poetic moments of Godunov-Cherdyntsev's idle observations as he strolls, like Kavalerov, through the Grunewald in *The Gift* [*Dar*][19] achieve their full richness not from a rapid succession of unexpected metaphors, passing from one object to another, but rather from their deliberate development. The proliferation of detail and metaphor functions as an instrument of insight into essence. The images are points on a circumference. They focus in contemplation of the object or state described. The observations are part of a carefully controlled

18 Vladimir Nabokov, preface to *The Eye*, p. x.

19 Vladimir Nabokov, *Dar*. Take for example the following passage in the Scammell-Nabokov translation: "And if I tilted my head back even farther, so that the grass behind (inexpressibly, primevally green from this point of upturned vision) seemed to be growing downward into empty, transparent light, I experienced something similar to what must strike a man who has flown to another planet (with different density and a different stress on the senses)—especially when a family out for a stroll went by upside down, with every step they took becoming a strange, elastic jerk, and a lobbed ball seemed to be falling—even more slowly—into a dizzy abyss." (p. 344)

and sufficient structure. Nabokov survived and flourished, nourishing himself on a self-created intellectual reality, feeling neither a thirst for the comradeship of Kronstadt sailors, nor the need to be loved by Soviet readers, indeed, feeling no need to be loved by any one at all.

Nabokov's self sufficiency is, however, unique. Not only Shklovskii, but also Tsvetaeva, Pasternak, Belyi, and even clever, cynical Erenburg left Berlin and returned to Russia. It was Il'ia Erenburg, more than any of the other representatives of the "westernizing trend" in Soviet literature, with whom Olesha was first, and often favorably, compared. A. Lezhnev felt that Olesha shared Erenburg's lightness of construction, transparency of thought, and easy sentimentality, but that he had much more taste and finesse than the older writer.[20] Lezhnev found a definite Erenburg influence not only on the style but also on the content of *Envy*, particularly in the Ophelia episodes, and cites the concluding scene where Ivan and Kavalerov drink to indifference at Annechka's as "a typical Erenburg ending: the dreamer with his nose in the dirt."[21]

Certainly *The Extraordinary Adventures of Julio Jurenito* [*Neobychainye pokhozhdeniia Khulio Khurenito*] and *Envy* are both novels of self-mockery as well as satires on vulgar materialism. Olesha's Kavalerov, fighting against the Utopia of the Quarter, is a worthy successor to the character named Il'ia Erenburg who protests to his teacher about the mechanization of life. Julio Jurenito tries to explain to his disciple Erenburg that the ecstasy of the New Man is "that of a mechanic who has just grasped for the first time the workings of a complicated machine."[22] Erenburg protests: "Teacher,

20 A. Lezhnev, *Literatura revoliutsionnogo desiatiletiia*, p. 80.

21 A. Lezhnev, *Literaturnye budni*, p. 217.

22 Il'ia Erenburg, *Neobychainye pokhozhdeniia Khulio Khurenito i ego uchenikov*, p. 296.

these new men you speak of are monstrous and therefore impossible. There is no chance in their lives, and therefore nothing wonderful; the unexpected, the contradictory, romanticism are all lacking. There's nothing there." (p. 297) The images of Jurenito's reply are the same as those Ivan Babichev uses in his parable of the garbage pit. Jurenito says:

[. . .] you're a man of the old species. [. . .] Old things always smell of rot and mothballs, but that stench is highly valued under the name of "romanticism." [. . .] Everything you're so anxious about, caprice, whim, is rotting fast, and soon it won't even assail your nose anymore. Of course, if you rent a separate room without neighbors you can weep over the past for the rest of your life, but that isn't likely to change anything. [. . .] If you start firing at the sun at dawn from a thousand batteries, it will rise anyway. Perhaps I hate this dawning day no less than you do, but in order that tomorrow may come, you must steadfastly meet the cruel sun, you must help mankind walk in its rays, and not cling to the cupola of some little old church on which formerly, yesterday, the dying sunlight gleamed. (pp. 297-98)

Ivan too speaks of thousands of years of culture piled in a dump hole, a dark bleak pit. "And rotten stumps, phosphorescent mushrooms shine in the pitmold. Those are our feelings! That's all that's left of our feelings, of the flowering of our souls. The new man will come to the pit, rummage around, climb down into it, pick out what he needs—maybe some machine part, or a wrench. But as for the rotten stump, he tramples it, extinguishes it." (p. 90) Ivan wants to "scratch history's mug" as he fades out, but Jurenito, the complete cynic, is resigned to the inevitable. He would never lead a "conspiracy of feelings." Erenburg's real nihilism enabled him to let go of those cupolas to which Olesha clung. At the very time that Olesha published *Envy*, Erenburg stated: "When I was younger I liked heroes with violent passions and outlandish emotions. In those days, I was interested in vices, poses, and adventures. But now I am impressed neither by the play of the imagination, nor by strength of character, nor by valor."[23]

Erenburg's detachment sets him somewhat apart not only from Olesha but also from the rest of that rather amorphous group of writers who shared as their basic theme the emotional difficulty of the old intelligentsia in adjusting to the Revolution and finding a role in it. Critics such as El'sberg, Lezhnev, and Kirpotin[24] have traced the history of these "fellow-traveler" writers from their first apprehension of the elemental fury of the Revolution, through their disillusionment and disgust at the NEP period,[25] to their subsequent attempts to deal in literature with the problem of the cultured individual, ultimately committed to a belief in the worth of his own individuality, emotionally isolated and alienated from the new regime. Olesha's *Envy* is usually considered a manifestation of the same fellow-traveler literature which brought forth Il'ia Selvinskii's "Pushtorg" and "Notebooks of a Poet" ["Zapiski poeta"], Leonid Leonov's *Thief* [*Vor*] and "The

23 Erenburg, *V Protochnom pereulke*, in *Sobr. soch. v deviati tomakh*, II, 483.

24 See Zh. El'sberg, "Nastroenie sovremennoi intelligentsii v otrazhenii khudozhestvennoi literatury," in *Krizis poputchikov*, pp. 7-68; A. Lezhnev, *Literaturnye budni;* V. Kirpotin, *Proza, dramaturgiia, i teatr*, particularly the chapter on Leonov; B. Ol'khovyi, "Eshche raz o literaturnom poputnichestve," *Pechat' i revoliutsiia*, No. 8 (1929), pp. 12-29; Iu. Lebedinskii, "Segodnia poputnicheskoi literatury i zadachi LAPP," *Zvezda*, No. 1 (1930), pp. 187-90.

25 In the category of protests against the drab reality and corruption of the NEP period, there are many works of underworld literature: V. Kataev's *Embezzlers* [*Rastratchiki*], Il'f and Petrov's *The Twelve Chairs* [*Dvenadtsat' stul'ev*] and *The Golden Calf* [*Zolotoi telenok*], A. Sobol's "Shadow Pictures" ["Kitaiskie teni"], and V. Kaverin's *The End of a Gang* [*Konets khazy*].

Leonov's Mitka Vekshin in *The Thief* [*Vor*] and Babel's Benia Krik are among the last incarnations of the Robin Hood figure whose passing from literature Olesha mourned in "Zametki dramaturga," p. 404.

End of a Petty Man" ["Konets melkogo cheloveka"], Konstantin Fedin's *Cities and Years* [*Goroda i gody*] and *The Brothers* [*Brat'ia*], and Kaverin's *The Brawler* [*Skandalist*] and *Artist, Unknown* [*Khudozhnik neizvesten*].

As the basic purpose of this chapter is to attempt to define the nature of Olesha's artistic imagination within the context of the 1920s rather than to write a history of that period, I shall confine my detailed discussion to Kaverin and Fedin, both of whom shared thematic and stylistic traits with Olesha and later managed to resolve the philosophical conflicts which obsessed them in the twenties.

All three, Fedin, Kaverin, and Olesha, were followers of Evgenii Zamiatin. Both Fedin and Kaverin were members of the Serapion Brotherhood.[26] They attended the courses Zamiatin gave on prose writing in the early 1920s. Although Olesha was not formally one of his pupils, Zamiatin exerted a considerable stylistic and thematic influence on him.

Olesha feared the same thing as did Zamiatin: the extirpation of whim and unpredictability by a conformist welfare state based on logic and "enlightened self interest."[27] In Zamiatin's novel *We* [*My*], the Well-Doer and the Guardians operate to remove the irrational faculty—called "fancy"—from the brains of the citizens of the Single State. They hope thereby to quell a rebellion aimed at restoring the unity of man's rational and emotional natures. Similarly, for Ivan

[26] A group of young writers, founded in 1921, and whose major doctrine was the belief that everyone should be able to write as he wished, free from any external literary control. Members were Zoshchenko, Fedin, Kaverin, Shklovskii, Slonimskii, Nikitin, Vsevolod Ivanov, Lunts, and Tikhonov.

[27] The influence of Dostoevskii's *Notes from the Underground* on Zamiatin's *We* has been discussed quite widely. See Jackson, *The Underground Man in Russian Literature*, and Richard Gregg, "Two Adams and Eve in the Crystal Palace: Dostoevsky, the Bible, and *We*," *Slavic Review*, No. 4 (December, 1965), pp. 680-87.

Babichev, prophet of a "conspiracy of feelings," "Fancy is the Beloved of Reason." (p. 77)

Even Olesha's color symbolism is like Zamiatin's in *We*. For instance, blue is the color of the uniforms and buildings of the Single State. Blue is also the color of the enemies of fancy in Olesha. Andrei Babichev demands that the color used in posters to advertise his food products be a dull, chemical blue, not a romantic pastel. (p. 30) The color-blind man who chides Shuvalov for "flying on the wings of love" is condemned to eat blue pears. ("Love," pp. 76-77) Zamiatin's desirable women wear light-colored dresses and their flesh glows rosily through the material. The same golden, rosy glow radiates through the pastel dresses of Valia and Shuvalov's mistress Lelia.

Olesha has appropriated to his own use many of Zamiatin's most characteristic stylistic devices: elliptical sentences, systematic distortion of visual images, and especially the use of what Shklovskii calls "the extended epithet":

> The device consists in the fact that a definite characteristic, something in the nature of an extended epithet, accompanies the hero throughout the entire work, and he is shown to the reader from that side only. If it is necessary to alter the hero, then the alteration is represented in the plane of the same original characteristic.
>
> For example, if the hero is defined as a tractor, then, when aroused, he will be compared to a tractor without a steering wheel.[28]

Olesha does not make consistent use of the extended epithet, but he adopts it for periods of limited vision: e.g., Kavalerov's images of Andrei Babichev as a monument or a mechanical idol in part I of *Envy*.

The first resemblance between Olesha and Kaverin and Fedin

[28] Shklovskii, "Potolok Evgeniia Zamiatina," in *Piat' chelovek znakomykh*, p. 50. Quoted in Alex M. Shane, *The Life and Works of Evgenij Zamjatin*, p. 151.

is thus their common debt to Zamiatin. There are, however, many other similarities, both of vision and technique, which link the three younger writers.

Fedin's first volume of stories, *The Wasteland* [*Pustyr'*], was about little men, lonely and isolated. What he says about them is very close to Olesha's statement that one must work out lizard themes. "The little man, the hero of *The Wasteland*, was the subject of my attention for a long period of time. [. . .] It was the outcome of my existence in the old literature, the result of my hermetically closed schooling, my hidden dreams. I had to give it birth or else this deadly fruit would have died within me—poisoned me."[29]

Cities and Years, published in 1924, was an extremely interesting attempt to grasp the complexities of the Revolutionary period by means of elaborately structured flashbacks and the gradual unveiling of the complex of reasons behind seemingly arbitrary events. The basic problem of *Cities and Years* is that of the passive intellectual, paralyzed by the contrast between the revolutionary ideal and the bloody activity it entails. Andrei Startsov (the root of whose name *star* means "old" in Russian) is finally doomed by his acquiescence in the demands of personal loyalties which lead him to free an enemy of the Revolution. Startsov is killed for this betrayal by his own friend and opposite, Kurt Wahn, who is both an artist and a Bolshevik.

Startsov defines his hopeless alienation from a world in total revolution in language which recalls Kavalerov's. He, too, wanted to be at the center of things, to "get in." Startsov also compares himself with a dog:

> I remembered how in winter I came across a little dog which was scratching at a closed door with its forepaws. [. . .] In scratching at the door the little dog had bloodied its paws.

29 Letter quoted in B. Brainina, *Konstantin Fedin*, pp. 47-48.

It couldn't understand that it wasn't at all needed in this world.

I understand it. About myself, that is. [...]

All my life I have tried to get into the circle. You understand, so that everything in the world would go on around me. But I always got washed away, carried off to one side.

I bloodied myself for nothing. [...]

In short, I gave up scratching....[30]

Fedin's next novel, *The Brothers,* is simpler in construction than *Cities and Years,* taking place largely in the less dramatic postrevolutionary period. Critics compared *The Brothers* with *Envy* because the basic situation of brothers set one against the other is very close to that of Olesha's novel.[31] Both novels have as their central character an intellectual-individualist opposed by "a builder of the present." In both novels a representative of the intelligentsia provides a link with the past. Fedin's Arsenii Arsen'evich Bach, a biologist, is a nonburlesqued Ivan. He declares to a "new man":

We don't know the beauties which you will create. We don't know how you will feel your new beauty. But our feelings will never be repeated because the man of our epoch will never be repeated. But we knew how to feel, Rodion, we knew how to create the beautiful and be seduced by it. And I am sad, Rodion, that the new men throw us out of life pitilessly. [. . .] We have in ourselves feelings you guard against not because they are harmful, but simply because you don't possess them and don't want to see their meaning. We carefully nurture a feeling for the past, but you uproot the very seed of that feeling in yourself. I stop beside a house built by Rinaldi, and my heart beats. [. . .] Oh, for us time doesn't exist. We are the contemporaries of all epochs, we are truly immortal![32]

[30] Konstantin Fedin, *Goroda i gody,* in *Sobr. soch. v deviati tomakh,* II, 12-14.

[31] See El'sberg's discussion "Tvorchestvo Fedina," in *Krizis poputchikov,* pp. 137-39.

[32] Fedin, *Brat'ia,* pp. 355-56.

There is even a Volodia figure in the novel, a "builder of the future," and a girl, the incarnation of the new, young and excellent world to which the intellectual aspires, but which is finally beyond his reach.[33]

The Brothers is closer to "The Notebooks of Fellow-Traveler Zand" than to *Envy* in at least one respect. The intellectual hero, Nikita Karev, is a creative artist, a composer. Thus, the basic problem of the novel is not merely the isolation of the intellectual but also an attempt to determine whether it is possible for a creative artist inevitably involved with the tradition of his art to function in the new world and be essential to it. Further, can the estrangement from the problems of "life" which creative art entails even be humanly or morally justified in the context of the Soviet 1920s?

Nikita Karev is selfish and isolated from the concerns of those around him. All his energies and emotions go into his *magnum opus,* and there is nothing left for human relations. Yet, he demands to be loved and to have his music loved, although he uses other people only to inspire the creation of his great symphony. According to Fedin's biologist, Arsenii Arsen'evich Bach, this symphony combines "the heroism of our day with the culture of the past." As Bach is an old intellectual, his opinion might not be representative. But the symphony is received favorably by an audience consisting not only of intelligentsia but also of sailors and other elements of the people. Fedin, therefore, posits the possibility of a successful contribution to a new socialist culture by an artist who is estranged from it by temperament and by the demands of his creativity. The final note is affirmative. If *The Brothers* by no means marked the end of Fedin's difficulties in successfully depicting a Soviet hero, it was nonetheless an extremely important step for him. Although the construction is less interesting

33 El'sberg, "Tvorchestvo Fedina," p. 137.

than that of *Cities and Years*, the occasional original comparisons and the careful use of color to express the mood of a scene are still very effective. Fedin was already moving toward a form acceptable both to himself and to the general Soviet public.

In order to say certainly how Fedin made his way to literary acceptability in the Russia of the 1930s, it would be necessary to analyze his life, works, and possible self-betrayals in as much detail as we have Olesha's. Nevertheless, one fundamental difference between these authors who have been compared so often is immediately obvious. Fedin is intensely serious. His satire, never light, is based both on a much greater first-hand knowledge of the terrible reality through which both Russia and Western Europe had lived between 1914 and 1922 and on a much greater concern with it. While Olesha strolled to high school in Odessa, carefully avoiding certain bad-luck stones in the sidewalks, and cheerfully playing hookey if he happened to step on one,[34] Fedin, interned in Germany, already an adult, watched the return of the mutilated wounded and the blatant hypocrisy of both sides in the struggle.

No one who has read the terrible, grotesque pages of *Cities and Years* which tell of the riot of the war cripples (led by the widow of a blinded, deafened soldier whose trunk, without arms and legs, had been kept "alive" for a time) can fail to understand how the separate experiences of these two authors influenced their different postures to the world. Fedin's fantasy had been curbed by an early moral anger at an adult world from which he did not attempt to retreat. The structure of his imagination, his artistic tone, had nothing finally in common with Olesha's deliberate attempt to remain a child.

Veniamin Kaverin, born in 1902 of a cultivated Jewish fam-

[34] Lev Slavin has remarked that Olesha actually kept this habit even during his last years of high school. See "Moi Olesha," in *Portrety i zapiski*, p. 8.

ily, was closer than Fedin to Olesha in tone, style, and vision. Kaverin's early works were written under the influence of E. T. A. Hoffmann and Edgar Allan Poe, the titular ancestors of that loose group of young writers who called themselves the Serapion Brothers. The volume of stories *Craftsmen and Apprentices* [*Mastera i podmasteria*] consisted of carefully wrought tales of adventure and fantasy much akin to *skazka*, where shadows could be exchanged or lost in the tradition of Peter Schlemil.

Although Kaverin retained a lifelong passion for this kind of literature, he soon turned his imagination to what he called the "abyss of romanticism" in his own contemporaries.[35] His "Summer Night" ["Vorob'inaia noch'"] is the story of the sort of little man Ivan Babichev exhorted to join his conspiracy of feelings. Kaverin's hero is similar to an Oleshan character:

> Among the cashiers of the middle stratum of the republic there are generally quite a few eccentrics and dreamers. Sitting in the locked circle of their fantastic gratings, letting huge sums of money through their hands, they are naturally inclined to dreaminess and ambition.
>
> It is precisely from among the cashiers that new Caesars and Bonapartes will emerge in our time. (p. 9)

Kaverin's cashier feels himself better educated and more intelligent than most men, perfect material for a brilliant but still only vaguely envisaged destiny: "Actually, Martin Matveevich had no clear idea of precisely what awaited him. In any case it would happen by *force majeure*—an unforeseen event, an unexpected and brilliant change. [. . .] Some kind of wonderful transformation waited in his future." (p. 13) A change does occur in his life, but quite unlike the one he had hoped for: he loses all the cooperative's money at cards. In

[35] Veniamin Kaverin, *Vorob'inaia noch'*, p. 7.

an attempt to get the money back by means of a blackmail scheme, Martin Matveevich is trapped into a "wedding" with an enormous hulk of a woman who plays a role similar to that of Annechka Prokopovich in *Envy*. The story ends with the hero fleeing barefoot, dressed only in his undershirt, and stoned by a crowd of pursuers:

> The unlucky man, lost, naked as the moon, was running along the streets of the town, and the Kaluga wind nipped at his heels like a stray dog.
>
> He ran, bent over, pulling his head into his shoulders, and the short undershirt flapped in hard pleats on his shoulders. [...]
>
> The disturber of the peace ran and ran and his heart beat like a drum during a public execution. (pp. 66-67)

In *The Brawler*, Kaverin moved on from the little world of the man who dreams of success and finds only disgrace to the intellectual world of St. Petersburg, but his biting, satiric tone remained the same. In 1930 he wrote *Artist, Unknown*, perhaps his most interesting novel, which is very close both in technique and theme to the early works of Olesha.

In the complicated structure of the novel, there are several different points of view. Some events are told to an unnamed author figure who writes them down as his various informants have seen them. Sometimes he finds out later that his informant has been "using the past as raw material" for a personal elaboration which does not correspond to the literal "facts" of a situation. But at the time of the first telling of any event, the Author records it as told. Sometimes he takes part in the events of the plot himself, as he is personally acquainted with the major characters. The Author, who has supposedly written the book we read, is at all times distinguished from its hero, Arkhimedov, the unknown artist of the title.

Arkhimedov, eccentric even in his "highfalutin" name,[36] dresses with a threadbare, nineteenth-century elegance recalling Ivan Babichev's "pretensions to elegance." Like Ivan, Arkhimedov is a street-corner prophet who is thrown in jail for his harangues. But Arkhimedov is in conflict with the new world not so much because it deprives him of the past but because it is inadequate to its own promise of a Communism which would be first and foremost a moral system, and which should be constructed from the beginning on the foundation of self respect. People must not spit in each other's faces. Workers must respect themselves and their responsibilities to the collective, modelling themselves on the example of the members of medieval guilds, punishing anyone who defrauds or cheats. Such romanticism, Arkhimedov asserts, may still be of use in the fight against insults, dishonor, hypocrisy, baseness, and boredom.[37]

Arkhimedov, who despairs of convincing adults and hopes to recruit an army of children, goes off to fight hypocrisy with his infant son (named after the German socialist, Ferdinand Lassalle) in his arms, and makes the prop room of the children's theatre his headquarters. The author realizes the justice of Arkhimedov's being in such a place, where make-believe is accepted as real, the past is living, and Arkhimedov can find depicted on the stage the honor, self-denial, and militant kindness he wants to exist in the real world.

36 The oddness of the name recalls Kavalerov's. It is appropriate to its bearer for a number of reasons. Arkhimedov wishes to re-establish a sense of honor modeled on that of a bygone day. His illustrious namesake kept the Romans at bay for a month by means of mirrors which set fire to their vessels. (Arkhimedov keeps theatre officials at bay.) Archimedes was killed by a Roman soldier who, not knowing who he was, became exasperated that Archimedes was too absorbed in what he was doing to answer the question put to him by a soldier of the New Order.

37 Kaverin, *Khudozhnik neizvesten* in *Sobr. soch. v shesti tomakh,* II, 67. Unless otherwise specified, page references are to this edition.

In such a theatre adults become like children once again and "enter the sphere of disinterestedness and nobility: sham falls from them like the skins shed by a snake." (p. 94) The Author himself experiences this return to purity when he accompanies two nieces to a performance of an adaptation of *A Tale of Two Cities.* In this state of temporarily renewed innocence, the noble figure of Sydney Carton, ready to sacrifice his own happiness and life for that of Charles Darnay, recalls Arkhimedov's friend and rival Shpektorov, a builder of Socialism, not Arkhimedov, to the author's mind.

We come to see that Arkhimedov lives in the atmosphere of the theatre but not of the play. Although he lives surrounded by the props of heroism, he speaks not to the children but to puppets hanging dumbly on the wall. His only other listeners are the stage manager and a certain Zhaba, a former linguist in whose mind names lived apart from objects, who rearranged the nomenclature of the world "as heedlessly as a woman, rearranging the furniture." (p. 89) Zhaba has temporarily become a very bad painter who wants to repaint the whole world. Even he realizes one evening that Arkhimedov's ideas will lead nowhere, when Arkhimedov, armed with Quixote's props, takes part in a hopeless battle with the enemy as represented by the director and officials of the theatre.

Zhaba is something of an artist, however, understanding and continuing to believe in the artistic ideas for which Arkhimedov continues to battle. "It is a fight for the integrity of one's eyes which will submit neither to laws nor to prohibitions." (p. 98) Arkhimedov's painting is "a new vision, the one which every artist great and small has been talking about for the past fifty years. It is the art of a man who fears nothing. Everything which other people consider banal, childish, laughable is of the utmost importance to him. He is the only artist of our time who is not afraid of morality." (p. 97)

Arkhimedov is finally seeking to regain purity of artistic vision and life in order to bring such freshness into the Soviet world. For "Arkhimedov lives by only one thing—the profound conviction that the new vision, for the sake of which he exists, is necessary to his time [. . .]" (p. 99) Arkhimedov is not just a character drawn in the archaic, prophetic tradition of Ivan Babichev. He is also depicted as an artist whose conception of his art and conviction that his vision is necessary to his time are fundamentally the same as Olesha's own attitude toward his art. Arkhimedov stands for childlike freshness of vision. He wanders through the city searching for colors, and the parts of *Artist, Unknown* which deal with Arkhimedov are written in a style very close to Olesha's, full of reflections, shadows, and brilliant light effects. The tone of the first episode is very Oleshan.

Shpektorov's profile, bisected by a blind, floated by in the dim glass of the shop windows, it scattered on the reflections of heads and shoulders which strode ahead independently and had left their now elongated, now foreshortened, legs far behind them.[38] [. . .]

A man with a trowel came out through the swinging door [revealing] a smoky movie frame which was momentarily reflected in Arkhimedov's glasses, with the mouths of people talking and drinking, hands stretched out toward glasses, an impatient silhouette by the telephone, a waiter, frozen in action, with his rocking tray—all the features of a vision like an interrupted dream.[39]

When the Author trails Arkhimedov through the city on his search for color, he sees him study effects of light and shade

[38] This image immediately recalls to mind the one of Andrei Babichev sailing down the glass porch in *Envy,* p. 112. Part of Kaverin's image has been cut from the version which appears in *Sobr. soch.* This quotation is therefore taken from the original version of *Khudozhnik neizvesten,* published in *Zvezda,* No. 8 (1931), p. 5.

[39] *Khud. neiz., Zvezda,* p. 6.

on the bottles in a drug store window, stand in front of a window whose perspectives change because of a swaying lamp inside, wander through the candlelit brilliance of a church service.

Arkhimedov is both a failure and a success. His wife Esther commits suicide by jumping from a window, his son rejects him and is finally adopted by Shpektorov, a builder of Socialism, with the Author's approval. In human terms, Arkhimedov has lost everything, he is destroyed. But this self-destruction turns out to be necessary to the creation of a painting, a primitive masterpiece whose content is the story of Esther's and his own destruction, a summation of all that Arkhimedov has seen and experienced.

The picture is described in a brief epilogue whose epigraph is a line from Khlebnikov: "and the storm blew right through the picture." The writer of the description, evidently a museum cataloguer, concludes:

> [. . .] only [an artist] who, in all the freedom of his genius, has overstepped the cautiousness and constraint of that painting which has become so estranged from people, could have succeeded in such a work. The mixture of lofty system with trifles, of commonplace details with a profound sense of time, this cannot be learned from masters, living or dead. Only an artist's vision boldly founded on what others consider fortuitous or banal could have determined on such a return to the child's view of the nature of things. Along with the unconscious force of imagination, intellect and memory are visible here—a terrible memory, perhaps based on a clear idea of what passes before the eyes of a man who is falling from a fifth floor [window]. One would have to be smashed to death in order to paint such a thing. . . .[40]

[40] *Khud. neiz., Zvezda,* p. 82. The *Sobr. soch.* text has the significant if small emendation "[. . .] only an artist's vision, boldly founded on what others consider fortuitous or banal, could decide on such a *return to the nature of things.*" (p. 154). Emphasis mine.

The person of the artist has been so totally destroyed to create this work that even Arkhimedov's name has been lost. The cataloguer concludes: "Oils, 80 x 120. Artist, unknown."

Kaverin ultimately affirms the artistic value of Arkhimedov's work of childlike authenticity, even though the artist and his family must be consumed to achieve it. Here he would seem to range himself alongside Olesha. But Arkhimedov is not the only artist in the novel. There is also the Author. Both his presence and the existence of the book written by him show that Arkhimedov's way is not the only one. Despite Arkhimedov, despite the complexity of Kaverin's literary technique, the development of the Author shows that in 1931 Kaverin had already found a way out.

The Author is no less an artist than Arkhimedov. His memories are no less vivid, his sensibility no less acute. Like Kaverin, he had once, "trusting to imagination," written "stories about Leipzig students who exchanged their shadows," (p. 116) and been an avid reader of Poe. He has read and refers to Mandel'shtam and Khlebnikov. Like Kaverin, he has just finished a book on Senkovskii. The Author is not only highly literate but also aware of developments in the pictorial arts. He knows and understands what Utrillo or the Cubists were about.[41]

The Author, then, is a maturing artist. He arrives at a stage where he feels an increasing need to clarify rather than to blur, to distinguish between illusion and reality. He goes to visit Shpektorov at a construction site in the steppe "so that in a place without illusions I might distinguish more clearly the

[41] It is perhaps worth mentioning that the Russian Cubo-Futurists, with whom Kaverin was familiar, were passionately interested in primitive and primitivist art. Zhaba has clearly been influenced by this Futurist interest as well as by Futurist theories of trans-sense language. The figure of Zhaba certainly owes something to those of Kruchonykh, and Igor Terentev, a painter-poet, *zaumnik,* and theatrical director, as well as to Khlebnikov himself.

border between life and dreams, failing which it would be very difficult to work and live." (p. 103) And there in the dust and heat he finds a man who wants to paint all the buildings different colors because he believes that grayness is one of the main causes for the decline of honesty, mutual confidence, and faith in the triumph of Socialism. Zhaba and Arkhimedov therefore have practical opposites who also aspire to "Socialist morality and beauty." In the course of the book, the Author evolves a viable alternative both to his own previous attitudes toward art and to Arkhimedov's. There is a distance maintained between him and Arkhimedov. It is clear, therefore, that despite striking similarities of texture, imagery, and thematic concerns, Kaverin's attitude toward *Artist, Unknown* is fundamentally different from Olesha's toward *Envy*. In 1931 Kaverin created both Arkhimedov and the Author. In 1931 Olesha was still an Arkhimedov, fighting desperately for the "integrity of his eyes" which would not submit to laws or prohibitions.

While Soviet critics have always compared Olesha with such fellow-traveler novelists as Fedin and Kaverin, they have tended to ignore Olesha's position as an epigone of the Russian Futurists. He shared with them many artistic devices and certain themes: a preoccupation with zoos, with *bouffes* for adults, and with the circus ring, where the laws of a stodgy and retrograde nature were challenged amid fanfare, bright lights, and even brighter colors. But Olesha himself participated neither in the formation of the Futurist movement and the elaboration of its ideology nor in the outlandish activities which were essential to its theory. He did not share the Futurists' messianism. He merely used for his more limited revolt the techniques and forms of the Futurists' revolution.

Although Olesha had many personal contacts with Maiakovskii and other Futurists after the Revolution, he was always aware that he was only a late-comer to the fringe of the movement.[42] He recalls when the Futurists came to Odessa during their first scandal-provoking tour of Russia in 1913 and 1914: "At that time, I wasn't yet a poet. I still lived only for soccer, a sport which had just begun to be played in our country. [. . .] True, at that time I had already translated the introduction to Ovid's *Metamorphoses* and got a five in Latin for it. . . . But I was still deaf to the miracle which was happening beside me—the birth of Maiakovskii's metaphor." (*Ni dnia,* p. 143) When Olesha was still an adolescent, Maiakovskii was already crowned with a fame bordering on notoriety. His impressive physique was made even more startling by the outrageous trappings which were part of the Futurist posture. The Futurists' theatricality and personal exhibitionism were an integral part of their revolt against bourgeois caution and decorum both in life and art. They proclaimed the total rejection of the hallowed past in the name of a fearless modernism: a new art for a new man.

The Poet, prophet of this new art, was inevitably subject to the scorn of the vulgar. In the tradition of the great, self-proclaimed poet-rebels, Maiakovskii saw himself inevitably martyred in the image of Christ, the Word made Flesh, by those who did not wish to hear.[43]

> This led to my Golgothas in the halls
> Of Petrograd, Moscow, Odessa and Kiev,
> where not a man
> but
> shouted:
> Crucify him!

42 Angelo Maria Ripellino in his extremely interesting *Majakovsky e il teatro rosso d'avangardia* tends to refer to Olesha as though he were more or less a Futurist. All my references to Ripellino's book will be to the French edition, *Maiakovski et le théâtre russe d'avant-garde.*

43 Lawrence L. Stahlberger in his *The Symbolic System of Majakovskij,* has remarked on Maiakovskii's predilection for Biblical references—the flood in *Mystery Bouffe,* the city as the work of Cain, etc. (pp. 53-55).

But for me—
all you people
even those that harmed me—
You are dearer, more precious than anything.
I am where pain is—Everywhere;
on each drop of the tear flow
I have nailed myself on the cross.[44]

In *Vladimir Maiakovskii—a Tragedy* [*Vladimir Maiakovskii —Tragediia*] the Old Man with the Cats says to Maiakovskii:

I am an old man who has lived a thousand years.
And I see—in you, on a cross of laughter
A tortured cry crucified.[45]

Maiakovskii is not a meek Christ but a rebellious one, demanding loudly to be crucified, taking on the whole world and God himself. For Futurism demanded that the world itself, the first creation, be broken down into components so that a new art might be created from these basic elements.[46] Poets like Khlebnikov decomposed words, making new ones from known roots and morphological elements, in order to create a new "trans-sense" [*zaumnyi*] language. The experiments of the Futurist poets moved along lines very similar to those of the painters who were their co-workers and contemporaries. It is significant that Burliuk and Maiakovskii were also painters, that Khlebnikov and Kruchonykh were extremely interested in the problems of painting, and that the painters Filonov and

[44] Maiakovskii, "Oblako v shtanakh," trans. Max Hayward and George Reavey in *The Bedbug and Selected Poetry*, ed. Patricia Blake, pp. 83-85. This poem was originally to have been called "The Thirteenth Apostle" ["Trinadtsatyi apostol"].

[45] *Vladimir Maiakovskii—Tragediia,* in *Sobr. soch. v chetyrekh tomakh,* I, 78.

[46] Stahlberger, p. 60.

Malevich[47] also experimented with poetry. Kruchonykh wrote in *The Word as Such* [*Slovo kak takovoe*]:

> The Futurist painters like to use anatomical parts, cross sections of organs, and the Futurists who are the creators of a new language [use] broken words, amputated words from which they draw clever and extravagant combinations (trans-sense language). In this fashion one may obtain the greatest possible expressive force. That is what distinguishes the language of our impetuous era, the language which has killed the frozen language of a previous time.[48]

Thus, both poets and painters deliberately fragmented the world in their art. They broke and mixed objects in order to create a modern art that was "an organized violence practiced on nature."[49]

As Lawrence Stahlberger has noted in his book *The Symbolic System of Majakovskij*, the images of Maiakovskii's poetry, always highly visual and pictorial, are often based on such distortion and wrenching of objects. They appear in violent movement, in a tumult appropriate to the pace of a modern poetry patterned on the contemporary city.[50] Maiakovskii declared in a speech in Nikolaev on January 24, 1914:

> Futurist poetry is the poetry of the city—of the modern city. [. . .] The city itself is becoming an element from whose womb a new, urban man is being born. [. . .] We city dwellers don't know the

47 Malevich later disassociated himself from the Futurists because they had not gone far enough in freeing art from the object. In his 1915 manifesto "From Cubism to Suprematism" ["Ot kubisma k suprematizmy"], he declared: "In unpacking all objects, the Cubo-Futurists have broken but not burnt them." (Quoted in Ripellino, p. 40.)

48 A. Kruchonykh and V. Khlebnikov, *Slovo kak takovoe*, p. 12. Olesha, unlike Kaverin, never speaks of these painters, only of Gustave Doré, Tiepolo, Delacroix, etc.—the painters of a bygone romanticism. The only time Olesha speaks of modern painting is a vague reference in a description of Maiakovskii: "a youth in a velvet, un-Russian blouse [. . .] writing verses clearly inspired by French painting. [. . .]" (*Ni dnia*, p. 144)

49 Stahlberger, p. 60.

50 *Idem.*

forests, fields and flowers—we are acquainted with the tunnels of the streets, their movement, noises, rumbling, flickering, eternal circulation. The most important thing is that the rhythm of life has changed. Everything has become lightning-fast, swift as it is on motion picture films. The flowing, calm, unhurried rhythms of the old poetry don't correspond to the psyche of the modern city dweller. The tempo of our day is feverish. There are no flowing measured, curved lines. The picture of the city is one characterized by corners, fractures, zigzags. Poetry [. . .] must correspond to the new elements of the psychology of the modern city.[51]

The disintegrated urban world of *Envy* is obviously created in the same modernist rhythms. The city can be terrifying because it is the epitome of the non-natural. It is in itself a fantastic distortion of nature, a seeming contradiction of natural law in the simple sense of man living in harmony with earth and sky and the slow cycle of the seasons. Thus, the city gives rise to nonnatural conceptions born of this dislocation.

Maiakovskii's poetry attempts to find a new structure which can take this dislocation into account. Particularly appropriate to an attempt at the creation of a new poetry for the hallucination-inducing city is the device of the realization of metaphor: taking a metaphor literally within the context of the work of art. Roman Iakobson in his *New Russian Poetry* [*Noveishaia russkaia poeziia*] says that the transformation of a poetic trope into a poetic fact is the characteristic device of the poetry of Khlebnikov and Maiakovskii.[52] Maiakovskii's tragedy *Vladimir Maiakovskii* is full of such materializations. Abstractions become clothes, kisses blow up into rubbery cushions which lie around the stage and can be worn like galoshes. Such a literary device is particularly apt for translation into cinematic terms. To take only a few examples from one of Maiakovskii's scenarios *How Are You?* [*Kak pozhivaete?*],

[51] In V. Katanian, *Maiakovskii, literaturnaia khronika*, 4th rev. ed., p. 56.
[52] Roman Iakobson, *Noveishaia russkaia poeziia*, p. 15.

the letters out of which Maiakovskii is making a poem start to fly around the room. Maiakovskii catches them on his pencil and dumps them on the paper where they mix with the ones already there to form lines from other poets' poems. After separating the rebellious letters, Maiakovskii jumps into a newspaper to save a girl from committing suicide. When he and the girl fall in love, they grow airplane wings with which they fly up the stairs into a room in which everything begins to blossom—lilies even grow out of the ink well.[53]

The realized metaphor of "flying on the wings of love" immediately calls to mind Olesha's "Love." In fact, Angelo Mario Ripellino in his book *Maiakovski et le théâtre russe d'avant-garde* explicitly compares Olesha's technique with Maiakovskii's[54] The equivalence is only superficial, however. As we have seen, Olesha almost always undercuts metaphors. He never allows them to be "realized." Even Ophelia's real existence is hedged around with "perhaps." She actually appears only in dreams and in the tales told by Ivan Babichev. A

[53] Ripellino remarks that the scene recalls Chaplin's dream in *The Kid* in which a slum becomes a wonderful country festooned with roses, while the people there grow wings. (p. 320) The device of objects which blossom or fade according to the fortunes of characters has been used more recently, and extremely effectively, in Boris Vian's novels, particularly in *L'Ecume des jours,* where the wonderful apartment of Cleo and Colin into which the sun streamed like diamonds begins first to round at the corners, then gets smaller and damper and more opaque as Cleo sickens. After Cleo dies, the pet gray mouse has just time to scuttle out under the door before the apartment snaps shut altogether and disappears.

[54] *Ibid.,* p. 317. Ripellino does not refer to "Love," however, but to *Envy.* "The ringing of bells materializes in the form of a personage made of sound, and named Tom Virlirli." Olesha's device may seem similar to Maiakovskii's becoming a bear and floating down a river of tears, or to someone putting on a kiss like an overshoe, but the contexts are so different as to change the meaning of the device. The materialization of Tom Virlirli is both explicable and destructive of Kavalerov's fantasy. He need not imagine himself as Tom Virlirli, because Volodia Makarov, who appears at the door, home from his vacation, is the only possible incarnation of this dream in the Soviet world.

materialization is not allowed to stand as such and take up a real existence within the context of the work of art. Even in "Love," a story which takes place while the hero is in an "abnormal" state and subject to hallucinations, Shuvalov does not grow wings, and the phrase "flying on the wings of love" appears as the explanation of Shuvalov's odd state rather than as the understood source of a realized metaphor.

The real differences behind the superficial similarities between Maiakovskii's and Olesha's techniques become even clearer if one examines the nature of metamorphosis in their works, particularly the animation of inanimate objects. In *Vladimir Maiakovskii* pianos bite and chimneys dance:

> And suddenly
> all the objects
> stampeded
> tearing their voices
> to rip off the rags of worn-out names. [. . .]
> From the tailor, dead with fear,
> trousers have fled.
> They went—
> alone!
> without human thighs!
> Drunk—
> its maw gaping black—
> the bureau has fled from the bedroom.
> The corsets climbed down, afraid of falling,
> from the 'robes et modes' signs.
> Each galosh is inaccessible and severe.
> Coquettish stockings
> wink come-ons.
> I flew like a curse.
> My other leg
> is still running a block back.[55]

[55] *Vladimir Maiakovskii*, pp. 86-87.

Ripellino has a point when he declares that the revolt of objects described here and elsewhere in Maiakovskii inspired the familiar passage in *Envy*:

Things don't like me. Furniture tries to trip me up. Once the polished corner of some thing literally bit me.[. . .] If some piece of junk—a coin or a collar button—falls off the table, it usually rolls under some hard-to-move piece of furniture. When, crawling around on the floor after it, I raise my head, I see the sideboard laughing.[56]

Certainly both writers, as well as almost all other avant-garde artists, were aware of the danger that modern life would become ruled by the object, that man was threatened by the things he had made. But things are not exclusively malevolent in *Vladimir Maiakovskii.* When the Old Man with the Cats says, "You see / We must chop up objects / I was right to sense the enemy in their caresses," another character says "Perhaps one should love objects? / Perhaps they have a different soul."[57] In *How Are You?* during the love scenes, objects do everything in their power to become more agreeable. They are even capable of returning the love of a poet who loves them.

In Maiakovskii's work everything may be affected by metamorphosis. Even the poet is not exempt from these transformations. Not only do inanimate objects become animals, the poet becomes an animal himself. Olesha's hero on the other hand, is never transformed into anything else.[58] He observes, but does not participate.

Maiakovskii becomes an animal involved in the action: a

56 Ripellino, p. 65; *Zavist'*, p. 26.

57 *Vladimir Maiakovskii*, p. 81.

58 Only once, in a fit of despair, does Olesha even *compare* himself to an animal, and then it is simply to say that on his face there is a dog's snarl, not that he is a dog. ("Ia smotriu v proshloe," p. 291.)

dog being abused, a bear carried on a flood of tears, very often a bull tormented by the yoke or baited in the ring, as in "The Backbone Flute" ["Fleita-pozvonochnik"]:

> Inserting a smile in your lips,
> you will look
> and see a fine toreador!
> And suddenly I,
> from a bull's dying eye,
> will fling my jealousy into the boxes.[59]

As we have noted in a slightly different context, Olesha's sympathies are with the intrepid Torero, a handsome hero in delicate control of a dangerous brute force. Maiakovskii identifies with the elemental strength of the tormented bull.

The difference is not fortuitous. It betrays the fundamentally different attitudes the two writers held as to the role of the poet. Maiakovskii's *I* is that of the Poet: a persona of the universal Artist, a possessor of a force which can change the world. His individual *I* is committed to a struggle of cosmic importance in which it may ultimately be a casualty. Olesha's *I* stands only for Iurii Karlovich Olesha. It watches from safety. Maiakovskii is totally committed: his poetry is a question of life and limb. He sees himself as a tightrope walker with only his own soul for support: "Over the abyss I've stretched my soul as a tightrope, and juggling with words, totter above it."[60] Olesha never sees *himself* as the tightrope walker, but rather as a member of the audience enviously watching someone else's daring.

In the end, Olesha cannot risk his individuality. He is not an artist in order to be metamorphosed with his time and to sacrifice himself for his art. He is an artist precisely so that

59 Maiakovskii, "Fleita-pozvonochnik," in *The Bedbug*, trans. Hayward and Reavey, p. 121.

60 *Ibid.*, p. 125.

his personality may remain safe in a world in convulsion. He shares Kavalerov's joy in the mirror of a modernist art where: "Your face hangs immobile in the middle of the mirror. It alone has kept its natural shape; it alone is a particle which has been preserved from the regular world while everything else has collapsed, changed, and acquired a new regularity to which you will never become accustomed [. . .]" (p. 71) And that, for Olesha, is the whole point of being a writer.

Olesha felt a profound affinity to Aleksandr Grin. They had both nourished their childhoods with the works of Mayne Reid, Edgar Allan Poe, and E. T. A. Hoffmann; both dreamed of liberation from everyday constraints and felt the need to create a more "radiant world" in their art.

Shortly after Grin's death in 1932, Olesha wrote:

> I knew Aleksandr Grin personally and spent many hours with him. I experienced very complex feelings when I was with him. Whatever we talked about, no matter what was the object of my attention, I couldn't stop thinking that a most extraordinary man was sitting before me. A man who could invent [*vydumyvat'*].
>
> I'm a writer too, but here, I thought, sits a writer of a completely special kind. He invents things which might be popular legends. This man invents the most amazing, tender, and simple kind of literature: *skazka.*[61]

A brief study of the nature of Grin's imaginative creation, which Olesha judged to be of a higher nature than his own, provides a helpful sidelight on the ambivalence of Olesha's artistic imagination.

Olesha's adolescence and young manhood were relatively sheltered; Grin's were almost as fabulous as Gorkii's. As a boy in Viatka, Grin dreamed of the sea, the rigorous life of simple comradeship, unknown dangers, and long voyages to strange

61 "Lit. tekhnika," p. 433.

lands. Olesha's equivalent longing was the more civilized desire for a bicycle trip through the cities of Europe, although he too felt a reverence for sailors as being from an unknown and strenuous world.

Grin was not content merely to dream. He ran away to Odessa where he tried doggedly to sign on any ship that would have him. He was imprisoned and exiled for political activity, escaped, and wandered around port cities, became a soldier, led the life of a hobo.[62] During his last years he was almost penniless and often drunk. Yet, throughout this difficult existence he retained a certain childlike purity and trust, and, almost till the end, a powerful imagination.[63]

When the Revolution came, Grin rejoiced. But Paustovskii, who esteemed him highly, noted that Grin was one of those people who suffered from

> a constant, almost childlike impatience, a desire to see the final result of great events immediately. The realization that there was still a long way to go, that the reconstruction [*perestroika*] of life is a lengthy business, all that vexed Grin. [. . .]
>
> If the Socialist system could have blossomed as in a fairytale, overnight, Grin would have been overjoyed. But he could not and did not want to wait.[64]

62 This early period of Grin's life is recounted in his "Autobiographical Tale" ["Avtobiograficheskaia povest' "] *Sobr. soch. v shesti tomakh,* VI, 228-361.

63 In his "V chem volshebstvo Aleksandra Grina?," a postface to Grin's *Zolotaia tsep'*, and *Doroga nikuda,* Dmitrevskii recorded a conversation with Grin in 1930 wherein Grin tacitly admitted that his imagination was failing him. They were walking along the docks, and Grin said of a tugboat they saw: "It's just an ordinary tugboat . . . though on a night like this it should really be a corvette under full sail. But I don't see those sails now. However hard I try, I don't see them." (p. 387)

64 Konstantin Paustovskii, "Zhizn' Aleksandra Grina," introductory article to Grin's *Izbrannoe,* pp. 4-5. Paustovskii's description would apply very well to Olesha, who said, "The most important characteristic of my soul is impatience," (*Ni dnia,* p. 11) and it accurately describes the dilemma of the hero in Olesha's "Prorok."

Paustovskii goes on to say that Grin therefore tried to retreat from reality, considering that it was better to live in dreams than in the filth of a humdrum existence. Paustovskii's judgment is unfair to Grin on several counts. It ignores the tenacity which was one of Grin's most striking characteristics. Grin pursued for years his dream of going to sea. Sickly as he was, he taught himself to swim in waters that were dangerous even to skilled swimmers. He escaped from exile. His artistic imagination elaborated a whole continent with a consistent geography, and a shoreline dotted with individualized cities.

Even the *skazka* Grin invented was of a peculiarly strenuous kind. In it, things do not blossom overnight; they have to be planted and carefully tended. Grin's male characters believe they must create their own miracles. At the end of *The Golden Chain* [*Zolotaia tsep'*] the youthful hero says when asked what he desires: " 'I'm a sailor,' I said. 'I've gone a way along that road, anyhow. If you make me the master of a ship, I don't think I need anything else; I'll get all the rest myself.' "[65] In "The Heart of the Wilderness" ["Serdtse pustyni"],[66] Steele has been told a cock-and-bull story of a wonderful and happy community in the midst of the jungle, and he sets out to find it. The settlement does not exist, but it should; so the hero builds it. The construction takes a year. The search for the right people to live in it takes even longer. Steele has taken a dream seriously, and by working at it finally made it real.

It is true that "chance" does play a considerable part in the meetings and lives of Grin's characters. But chance is a constant element in any man's life: "Chance . . . chance! [. . .] There are many chances. A man makes friends by chance, makes decisions by chance, finds or loses something by chance. Every day is full of chances. [. . .] But it's worth

[65] *Zolotaia tsep'*, p. 91.

[66] First published in *Krasnaia niva*, No. 14 (1923). Reprinted in *Sobr. soch.*, IV, 329-36.

it to have the kind of chance occur which touches a man's very foundations. . . ."[67] The point is that chance may be acted on or let pass by forever. It depends on the kind of person one is, and whether one's soul seeks "a living fairytale," or tranquility.

Thus, in Grin's "Scarlet Sails" ["Alye parusa"], "Grey and Assol' found one another 'by chance' as educated people say, on the morning of a summer day full of inevitability."[68] Then Grey experiences great trouble and danger to fit out his ship, *The Secret,* so that it exactly fulfills the lifelong dream of Assol', a girl whom all the village scorns as a simpleton because she still believes a tale she had heard as a child that one day her beloved would come for her in a white ship with scarlet sails. Grey has "understood a simple truth. One must make so-called miracles with one's own hands."[69]

Thus, Grin's impatience implies neither a refusal nor an inability to work for something, only a disgust with pettiness and with the representatives of a self-renewing, soulless bureaucracy which, communist or capitalist, must oppose any innovation which threatens its existence. In *The Radiant World*, the representatives of the state wish to destroy the hero, a man who can fly, not only because he can look down from above and learn the secrets of forts and factories, but also because as an image of unheard-of "possibility" he is dangrous to all the entrenched structures of the status quo.

If Grin has remained popular among adolescents in the Soviet Union, it is largely because his stories are pervaded by the belief in this *possibility* incarnate in the pure of heart.

67 *Doroga nikuda,* p. 241.

68 "Alye parusa," *Izbrannoe,* p. 142.

69 *Ibid.,* p. 156. V. Vikhrov notes in his "Rytsar' mechty," the introductory article to Grin's *Sobr. soch. v shesti tomax:* "This story was conceived during the Revolution when the people were doing miracles with their own hands." (p. 31).

Grin's images became a part of the mental system of the rebellious youths of the early 1960s who wished to free themselves from hypocrisy in the name of something undefined but clean. The hero of Vasilii Aksenov's novel *It's Time, My Friend* [*Pora, moi drug, pora*], speaking of himself as he had been several years previously when he had first fallen in love with the girl who is now divorcing him, says: "What a guy I was: a wiseacre who had read all of Grin; I got high on the prospect of our perpetual life together—you and I, from North to South, East to West, two tramps with loving hearts [. . .]"[70] Of one of his friends, Kianukuk, the narrator says: "From that day on, Kianukuk began to await the arrival of the Mother ship of the fishing fleet. He stared at the whitish horizon and waited for it the way one always awaits the arrival of a ship—just like Assol'." (p. 126)

Born of an age of deceit, Aksenov's heroes adhere to Grin's morality of total individual honesty and sincerity. The peculiarly adolescent atmosphere of both Grin's and Aksenov's novels is due to the immediate establishment of relationships of trust.[71] Grin's whole imagined world is based on the assumption of the possibility of meaningful human contact. This does not mean that all people are seen as kind and good. In Grin's world, as in Aksenov's, there are two camps: the humane and imaginative versus the soulless and cruel. Even Grin's heroes are often destroyed in the struggle. As Olesha observed: "[. . .] that hint of irritation that permeates his stories—and

[70] Aksenov, *Pora*, p. 5.

[71] Grin's heroes are often adolescents or very young men. The heroines who truly understand them are also young. The atmosphere is often similar to such other creations of a poetic adolescent world as Alain-Fournier's *Le Grand Meaulnes.* Claude Frioux in his "Sur deux romans d'Alexandr Grin," *Cahiers du Monde Russe et Soviétique* (October-December, 1962), pp. 546-63, states that the adolescent paradise is Grin's exemplary myth: that, after having looked for the model attitude toward life in many traditional types of dreamers, Grin finally finds it in the adolescent sensibility. (p. 562).

that hint is unquestionably there—is because of Grin's disappointment that people were not as magically strong as they seemed to him in his imagination." (*Ni dnia,* p. 231) Olesha's comment provides a clue to the fundamental difference between the two writers. The first impulse of a Grin hero is to love and respect people, to expect the best. An Olesha hero is always more sophisticated. He operates on the assumption of lack of contact, not expecting to find comprehension and kindness. Actually, he does not expect to find people to share his dreams because he himself has very little confidence in their realization. He does not want help and encouragement; he wants sympathy.

Grin's works always emphasize aspiration, not degradation. In *The Golden Chain* [*Zolotaia tsep'*], Grin's imagination builds a palatial structure which is the realization of the aspirations of Ganuvar, "whose soul demanded a living fairytale." This creation of a palace requires nothing "impossible" to occur. But in other works Grin turns to more archetypal symbols of human fulfillment through the will to the attainment of "the Unrealized" [*Nesbyvsheesia*], as he does in *She Who Runs on the Waves* [*Begushchaia po volnam*].

This novel is both the story of a sleek vessel christened *She Who Runs on the Waves* and of Frezzi Grant, its namesake. The legendary Frezzi Grant jumped overboard from a frigate and ran across the crests of the waves to an incredibly beautiful island. She and the island were then swallowed up in the mist. Occasionally Frezzi Grant is seen again, bringing comfort to shipwrecked mariners. Thomas Harvey, cast adrift at night in the ship's launch by the captain of *She Who Runs on the Waves*, is joined by an unknown woman (later identified as Frezzi Grant) who suddenly appears on the ship's deck and demands to be put in the launch with him. After reassuring him that he will be picked up by a ship that will pass in the morning, Frezzi Grant leaves, running across the tips of the darkened waves.

The various manifestations of *She Who Runs on the Waves* develop into a complex symbol, a web of sounds and hints each of which must be followed in order to catch "the 'Unrealized,' the mysterious and wonderful stag, the quarry of an eternal hunt."[72] The entire complicated plot serves the central action of Harvey's attainment of knowledge of the Unrealized—a knowledge accessible to all who admit the power of the human spirit to run dry shod across the water.

In *The Radiant World* the same kind of "miracle" occurs. The hero, Drud, builds a light plane which flies by means of the vibrations of tiny bells. The sleek bell-plane with its swan-like prow does actually fly. Thousands of people see it, and the miracle is given a real existence within the context of the novel. In fact, however, Drud does not need even the bell-plane. He can fly without assistance as men remember flying in dreams.[73] Drud announces that he will fly in a circus on a certain day. The acrobats, tightrope walkers, and jugglers (who seem to break the laws of nature while actually they only play with them), claim enviously that Drud is a charlatan. At first, Drud hovers so near the ground that it seems to

72 Grin, *Begushchaia po volnam,* in *Izbrannoe,* p. 243.

73 M. Slonimskii tells of a discussion he had with Grin about an early version of what was to become *The Radiant World:* "He saw the doubt on my face and began to argue that after all there was nothing improbable about a man taking off and flying. He explained to me that mankind had certainly known how to fly once and had flown. He said that people had been and certainly would be again different from what they are now. [. . .] He cited dreams of flight as a proof that man had flown once. He considered these dreams, which are familiar to everyone, to be the memory of an atrophied human capability. He maintained that the development of aviation was the result of man's aspiration to regain this lost ability to fly. 'And man will fly alone without a machine,' he declared." (Quoted in the notes to Grin's *Sobr. soch.,* III, 441.)

be an illusion. But then he soars: "and the spectacle ceased to be an illusion [*fokus*] and became a miracle [*chudo*]: something which we secretly await all our lives."[74] Few people can accept Drud's image for what it is: a promise of the potential of the human soul, the vast possibilities of life. Drud's gift is the power of wonder. For, as he says once to one of his faithful friends, "the sun, the waves, the ability to say I, I, I, are just as wonderful as a flying man."[75]

Most people in the novel feel the need to delimit Drud, to explain him and fit him into a category. Curiously enough, Olesha felt this same compulsion when he read the novel. He tried to classify *The Radiant World* as "only a fantasy":

> It is interesting that even Grin himself had a false conception of himself [. . .] he compared himself with the Symbolists. [. . .]
>
> When I told Grin of my delight at the fact that such a truly wonderful theme for a fantastic novel had occurred to him (a flying man!), he was almost offended.
>
> "What do you mean a fantastic novel? It's a symbolic novel, not a fantastic one! It's not about a man flying at all, but about the soaring of a soul!" (*Ni dnia*, pp. 231-32)

The misunderstanding is typical both of Olesha's own imaginative caution and his attitude toward art. Olesha admires Grin's authenticity, his ability to create a complete fantastic construct, which places Grin's work somehow on a higher imaginative level than his own holiday patchwork of illusions—a texture which would have hedged Drud's flight in metaphors to keep it safely on the level of illusion rather than miracle. Yet, Olesha seems to assume that Grin's world is merely a more successful evasion. Olesha automatically apprehends a flying man only as a symbol of negative release:

74 Grin, *Blistaiushchii mir*, in *Sobr. soch.*, III, 78.
75 *Ibid.*, p. 124.

liberation from the everyday. For Grin, however, he is an affirmation of the potentiality of the human spirit, of the communion of pure hearts, indeed a symbol of a whole potential system of human relations.

Olesha works through a kind of conditional, grotesque distortion of the realized. His constant undercutting of his metaphors, his perpetual "laying bare of the device," create a sophisticated and fundamentally negative fantasy. Grin's affirmation of the Unrealized and his creation of a totally consistent fantasy world testify both to his naïveté and his commitment to the power of art, to the realization of *skazka* even at the cost of the destruction of its creator. In his "The Making of Asper" ["Sozdanie Aspera"], for example, Doctor Gakker is willing to die for his creation. Gakker explains that he invents people, but cannot publicly admit his authorship because "[. . .] other people must not suspect that the phenomena which astonish them are nothing but works of art. Painting, music, and poetry create the internal world of an artistic imagination. That is certainly estimable, but less interesting than my creations. I make living people."[76] The people Gakker creates are not ordinary ones, of whom there are already quite enough in the world, but people who can hold the center of universal attention and make a strong impression as does a great work of art. For, as Gakker says, man's greatest need after sleep, food, and love is for the unusual. Unlike Ivan Babichev, Gakker does not hope to feed this need on the scandal of a crime of passion but on the positive romantic image of Robin Hood.

The narrator listens as Gakker explains how he "created" living legends. "Gakker's tale resounded like an echo of human power." In order to put the finishing touches on his creation

[76] Grin, "Sozdanie Aspera," *Sobr. soch.*, IV, 198.

of Asper, the idealized robber, Gakker must allow Asper to be killed. Asper's "reality" can be sealed only by the presence of his body—and the only body he has is that of his creator. The narrator objects:

> "But look, life is worth more than Asper, think of that, my friend."
>
> "I have a special attitude towards life: I consider it an art; art demands sacrifices; therefore, a death of this kind attracts me. Having died, I shall merge with Asper, knowing, unlike other authors who are unsure of the significance of their works, that Asper will live on a long time and serve as material for other artists, creators of legends about magnanimous robbers."[77]

Asper is killed: the artist has become his own creation, the unreal has been made real, fantasy has been inserted into reality. If Olesha turns life into art by making real things seem to occur fancifully, Grin turns life into an art which is often itself about art becoming life.

Thus, Olesha was not only less "romantic"[78] than Grin, but also less romantic than the Socialist Realist writers, whose insistence on depicting future potential as an aspect of present reality made them underestimate the complexities which retarded the realization of the radiant future. When we contrast Olesha's works with Grin's, we see once more the limiting importance of the conditions of Russia in the 1920s on Olesha's imagination. Olesha went for holiday strolls through Moscow; Grin was a voyager. Not only did Olesha "not want to turn his back on Russia and her problems";[79] he could not. Olesha

[77] *Ibid.*, p. 204.

[78] The word "romantic" is to be understood here in the peculiarly purposive Soviet sense, as defined in L. I. Timofeev, *Kratkii slovar literaturovedecheskikh terminov:* "The romantic artist seeks to express in his images what he wants to see in life, what should, in his opinion, be fundamental and decisive in life."

[79] V. Zavalishin, *Early Soviet Writers*, p. 299.

had neither the artistic daring to replace his Russia with a positively different reality nor the moral confidence to believe in the possibility of any real transformation of the condition of mankind. In the end, Olesha did not believe that man could fly.

Chapter VIII

A Last Work: No Day without a Line

Olesha's last work, *No Day without a Line* [*Ni dnia bez strochki*], published in book form[1] posthumously in 1965, is as characteristically a work of the post-Stalin period as *Envy* is of the Soviet 1920s. *No Day without a Line* must be seen in the context of the flood of memoirs and diaries, reminiscences of friends and enemies, which began to appear in the Soviet Union after 1956. These documents are evidence of the need to record one's own truth, and to rehabilitate the lives of others who could no longer do so for themselves, a need which was endemic among writers who had passed through thirty years of deviousness, cowardice, or silence.

No Day without a Line is a collection of small, lapidary texts: evocations of the past, notes on passages from other writers' books which had become part of Olesha's own life,

[1] Olesha, *Ni dnia bez strochki.* Large parts of *Ni dnia bez strochki* had appeared under the title "Iz literaturnykh dnevnikov" in *Literaturnaia Moskva,* II (1956), 721-51. Another selection containing some of the same texts appeared under the title, "Ni dnia bez stroki" [*sic*] in *Oktiabr',* No. 7 (1961), pp. 147-69, and No. 8 (1961), pp. 135-56. Selections from *Ni dnia* were also included in Olesha's *Izbrannye sochineniia,* 1956, and in the 1965 *Povesti i rasskazy* under the heading "Iz zapisei 'Ni dnia bez strochki.'" The book *Ni dnia bez strochki* contains some fragments which had not, to my knowledge, been printed before, and leaves out certain others, notably a paen of praise to Krushchev the Peacemaker on the occasion of viewing a newsreel of his enthusiastic reception in Paris. (*Oktiabr',* No. 8, pp. 155-56.)

brief, informal comments about creative problems. It is a book whose subject is survival:

Let the reader not think that this book, however much it may apparently seem to be made up of disparate pieces on various themes, is only strung out lengthwise. No, it's rounded: [. . .] the book even has a subject, a very interesting one. A man has lived and survived to reach old age. That's a subject indeed, an interesting, even a fantastic subject. (*Ni dnia*, p. 171)

This last, incomplete book is as important for its form as for its subject. Its flawed shape is symbolic both of the nature and of the limitations of Olesha's creativity.

No Day without a Line is made up of fragments, and Olesha wants it that way, declaring that only such a discontinuous work is really in keeping with the characteristics of "contemporary psychology": "Modern prose works can have a correspondingly contemporary psychological relevance only when they are written at one sitting. A meditation or a memory in twenty or thirty lines, a hundred lines at most—that's what a really 'contemporary' novel is." (p. 11)

Olesha assumes that the major characteristic of modern life is fragmentation of attention. He claims to be writing for the girl he saw reading *Anna Karenina* on the long escalator of the Moscow subway. The girl reads in snatches. The reading of one episode is separated by time and extraneous interruptions from the next. Olesha asserts that the same fragmentation of attention must apply to the writer and determine the size of his compositional units, the manner in which they are written, and the lack of any explicit structural connection between them.

The "contemporary novel" as Olesha understands it is therefore congenial both to his peculiar abilities and debilities. It allows him to work in brief periods of concentration on small, self-contained forms. In his later years Olesha was affected by a not uncommon inability to settle down to sustained work.[2] But from the beginning, he had always preferred to write in small forms, to move from careful observation of one object to another without making explicit the relation between them. He had always been aware that his work "grows by the accumulation of separate fragments, one could almost say of strophes."[3]

It is significant that Olesha should have made an analogy with a traditional form of poetry to characterize his own prose style. He knew that meaning was contained almost entirely *within* each fragment of his writing, not arising from the confrontation of fragments. It is therefore not tragic that Olesha died without ordering the succession of the units which compose *No Day without a Line*. It probably would have been little different from the book as it now stands.

What is striking in *No Day* is the care Olesha expended on each separate fragment. Let us take as an example one of the shorter ones (most are a page or less in length):

When I entered the church, I would see the statues of angels standing along the walls at the level of a second story. They were almost children, at any rate no older than I, in tight tunics through which their bodies were visible. As I moved forward towards the altar, a foreshortening occurred, and the angels, one after another, turned more and more away from me, and the last one seemed to me to have turned his face to the wall, crying, grieving for me, but not having the right to forgive me. (p. 98)

[2] Lidin declared: "He had very little of it [glory, money, success] in his life, mostly because of his lack of organization. He didn't know how to allocate time. [. . .] Subjects flowed one after another from the reservoir of his observations and his memory, but in most cases, none of it was carried through, remaining just projects, carcasses of the subjects not covered with flesh. He lacked the work habits necessary for a writer. He liked to stroll, to see people, have conversations. [. . .]" (*Liudi i vstrechi*, pp. 117-18)

[3] In an inquiry in *Na literaturnom postu*, No. 4-5 (February-March, 1929), p. 120.

This fragment is totally self-contained, built around a single illusion (characteristically, one where Olesha feels himself being looked at and judged by someone else). Not only the boy but the whole fragment moves in a definite direction, and it builds to a climax which it carries within itself. It has clearly been worked over and carefully polished. It is thereby typical of *No Day without a Line*.[4]

Viktor Shklovskii said about this book, "Olesha tested each word on his teeth to see if it were gold, looked at it through a magnifying glass, turned it this way and that before he set it in a sentence."[5] Shklovskii's image is revealing in that he describes Olesha as someone doing the work of a skilled artisan, fitting together small, hard units, trying to make something genuine, nicely proportioned, and permanent. There is no doubt that insofar as Olesha is trying to fix the incidents of his life in *No Day without a Line*, he desires to achieve such small lasting forms. On another level, however, Olesha really wants to rise clear of his dependence on fragmented forms. He is perfectly aware that *No Day without a Line* is not really a startlingly "contemporary novel," but he can write no other way, and his work on these isolated units at least assures him of the possibility of continued creative activity. He admits in *No Day*: "So what if I only write fragments and never finish the work? Still, I'm writing; it's still a kind of literature. [. . .] Perhaps someone of my psychological makeup can write no other way in a historical period such as the present one." (p. 11)

Olesha had to write. Writing was one of the great sensuous pleasures of his life: "The pleasure of working is the result of

4 This fragment is also typical when considered from the point of view of content. The hero is a child, pitied only by those powerless to help him, but who is already doomed. A child for whom there will be no forgiveness from the Powers that Be.

5 Shklovskii, introduction to *Ni dnia*, p. 4.

a whole series of factors. You feel physically healthier, you feel your blood flowing more regularly. You even begin to experience a sensation which resembles pride—a feeling of full value" [*polnotsennost'*].[6] The pleasure and a sense of fluidity are interdependent: "The pleasure disappears when you begin to 'compose.' [. . .] by that I mean the activity of hand and mind when the writer has sensed the exhaustion of his attitude towards the world, when he begins to use ready-made images which have not flowed through his own bloodstream. Then the life of the phrase dies, then the light of the word goes out."[7]

Olesha thinks of real creativity in terms of a flow, the overcoming of fragmentation. He does not want to be conscious of the "activity of hand and mind." Shklovskii may be right, but Olesha does not want to be a jeweler, dealing with words and images as though they were outside of and independent of him. What he desires is to regain the moment of *making*, the moment of creativity when the consciousness of both time and manipulation is lost.

The distinction in Olesha's mind between creative "making" and mere "composing" or working seems to correspond to a distinction we have already noticed in his works. In the successful ones like *Envy*, when he is writing well and easily, confident in his artistic power, Olesha is not uncomfortably conscious of himself doing the writing: he is not fighting with his creation as though it were something alien which has to be controlled at every instant. Nor does the reader constantly feel the author's manipulating presence. In other works, however, Olesha is straining, and the reader is made aware of the strain by the constant hints and reminders that the author is there, that the story is in his capable hands. Such reminders serve to reassure the author, if not the reader.

6 "Literaturnaia tekhnika," p. 430. Olesha also uses the word *polnotsennost'* to characterize the life of aviators in "Polet," p. 308.

7 "Lit. tekhnika," p. 430.

Certainly from the late 1920s on Olesha's writing had been largely "composing." Not only had he lost the pleasurable sensation of his blood flowing more strongly as he created images, but it had become physically painful, indeed almost impossible for him to sit down and write. The vocabulary he uses to describe the blockage of his writing is no longer one of flow, but of fragile angularity. Olesha speaks of his very sentences breaking, falling into fragments: "It is very hard for me to write a phrase in one sweep as it were, especially if the phrase is intended as the definition of some abstract notions. The phrase suddenly breaks, and I'm left hanging, holding on, let's say, by some piece of a subordinate clause." (p. 43)

Olesha did try to discipline himself and win back the pleasure of mastery by forcing himself to write something every day.[8] But these exercises accentuated his tendency to work in very small units, to rewrite a single passage incessantly before he could proceed to anything else. Thus, such exercises actually prevented flow, and trapped Olesha in fragmentation. Nevertheless, as they were all Olesha felt capable of writing at the time they provided the only chance at all for him to write and regain facility. If the passage from working to making is mysterious, it is none the less clear that only through working is there any hope at all of achieving the higher state. Olesha makes a curious analogy:

These notes of mine are nonetheless useful to me because they teach me how to wield a phrase. And in general, they train me to write, something I was once very far from being able to do. To sit down at a desk and take up a pen would have been very difficult for me—oh, almost impossible—as hard as stepping from being awake directly into a dream without having fallen asleep. (p. 111)

[8] Olesha began this practice in the early thirties. In response to an interviewer's question as to whether he had ever tried to discipline himself, Olesha replied that he had been experimenting with daily work in notebooks. The result was that he had discovered "much precious ore"—but there was no work ready. ("Guliaia v sadu.")

Such is the essential passage into Art. If, as Olesha has said, "When you begin to see into the center of things, then the words come by themselves,"[9] the corollary truth is that when words come by themselves one begins to see into the center of things. When consciousness of fragmentation—fragmentation of language itself as well as the split between the artist and his language—is overcome, the artist penetrates to that center whose form itself symbolizes wholeness.

Olesha had thus become terribly aware of the dangers inherent in the same discontinuity which formerly he prided himself in controlling. Now he watches his structures fall apart, and recognizes that his writing has become an attempt to recreate meaning and fit broken elements back together:

> I have completely lost my ability to write. To write one line after another in unbroken succession is becoming impossible for me. I compose separate lines. That's possible if you're writing poetry, but one cannot write prose, articles, dramas that way. I don't compose, striding forward; I write as if I were looking backward. I don't create, shading, structuring, pondering; I remember. It is as though what I intend to write had already been written. Written, and then had somehow fallen apart, and I want to gather the fragments again into a whole. Either I must get free of this complex, or just quit the whole business. (p. 51)

His writing is no longer a process of creation which culminates in the bringing forth of something new and unexpected; it is a salvage operation. His language and images are no longer alive, surging within his bloodstream; they are already fabricated, calcified, exteriorized. Olesha is condemned to a kind of delicate repair work, which has little in common with writing in its state of grace.

Olesha cannot "just quit," however. If tortured writing locks one in time, flowing writing enables the artist to overcome the

[9] "Literaturnaia tekhnika," p. 430.

threat of time. Fluent, free writing can have a ritual efficacy, allowing Olesha not only to reevoke the past but also to create an interpenetration of past and present. (p. 299) The creation of this interpenetration is the ultimate purpose of *No Day without a Line.*

Olesha, frankly placing his effort to overcome time under the aegis of Marcel Proust, declares, "These notes are all attempts to resurrect life; one wants desperately to restore its sensations." (p. 40) "I would like to go backwards through life the way Marcel Proust succeeded in doing in his time." (p. 59) Olesha does not, however, wish to imitate Proust's effort to transmit what Shattuck calls the "thickness of human time traversed."[10] He has no intention of attempting to emulate the long, complex process which in Proust culminates, after several thousand pages, in the realization of *Le Temps retrouvé.* Olesha is primarily interested in Proust's successful retrieval of *moments bienheureux* and in his evocation of childhood sensations:

> I too would have liked to go backwards through life the way Marcel Proust succeeded in doing in his time.
>
> How does he start? I don't remember. I think he starts with the magic lantern, and how he sees the movement of the luminous, translucent, varicolored image on the wall, over the door, on the doorknob, and how the body of the knight Golo coincided with the doorknob, and so on. (p. 59)

In his artist's pleasure at the striking visual effect of Golo, Olesha ignores the context of this image. *A la Recherche du temps perdu* does not actually begin with Golo, but with a complex evocation of the problem of going to sleep—a problem not confined to childhood. The novel slips imperceptibly from waking to sleeping to waking, from Combray to Balbec to Paris, and raises the problem of not knowing *who* one is

[10] Roger Shattuck, *Proust's Binoculars,* p. 113.

because one doesn't know immediately on waking *where* one is. One may think one is one's eight-year-old self and then find oneself in Venice! Childhood is thus initially evoked in concomitance with later experiences. Furthermore, Golo appears as a menacing image. His presence in Marcel's bedroom, his transformation of Marcel's doorknob, does not give rise to joyful surprise, but to anguish: Golo destroys the slowly built up habit which alone makes the room bearable. The theme of habit, how it is broken and how it develops, recurs cyclically and significantly throughout *A la Recherche du temps perdu.* But Olesha is not really concerned with Proust's larger effort. He is interested in Golo as the image of an aesthetic perception produced by an optical illusion.[11] The re-evoking of such impressions in a work of art represents for Olesha a successful effort to lift them free of time. It is this goal which Olesha tries to achieve in *No Day.*[12]

Olesha insists that the memories of his life are particularly sacred because his is an artist's life. His body is host to an incomprehensible talent, a ruined athlete who stirs within him.

Sometimes I manage to hear what he is saying. I repeat it, and people think I'm clever. . . . Pasternak listens to me, as I notice, with pleasure. He listens to *me*, to the author of only two hundred-odd pages of prose, and he flushes, and his eyes sparkle. It's the genius, the broken statue stirring within me, in its chance envelope,

[11] As Shattuck remarks, most of the many optical illusions in Proust are there to show us the error of our perceptions, the distortion which occurs, and thus our distance from the truth. (p. 18)

[12] There is another way in which Proust's emphasis is significantly different from Olesha's, Proust declares that his book is to be a magnifying glass through which his readers will be able to read in themselves: "De sorte que je ne leur demanderais pas de me louer ou de me dénigrer, mais seulement de me dire si c'est bien cela, si les mots qu'ils lisent en eux-mêmes sont bien ceux qu j'ai écrits." (*Le Temps retrouvé,* in *A la Recherche du temps perdu,* III, 1033.) Olesha wants his readers to look at him, not at themselves.

expressing together with it the result of some strange and terrible enchantment, some detail of a myth from which I can understand only one thing—my own death. (p. 170)

Not only does Olesha visualize his talent as a body separate from his own, although seemingly trapped within it, but by 1956 he also sees this talent as broken, fragmented, only occasionally still managing to express itself through him.

The stirrings of this talent do become clearer as Olesha writes. Writing is therefore the central activity of his life which he thus tries both to preserve and to recreate. Not only does writing "settle accounts with memory," it also stirs up memory and brings back to the surface of consciousness moments and experiences which, forgotten, were as if they had never been. The process of writing sets into motion a vast information retrieval system:

When one writes, one feels an enormous, very complex, and mysterious machine at work within oneself. Some kind of levers on this machine extract memories and bring them to the surface. When you are wielding your pen and thinking, say, about syntax, you feel at the same time a memory begin to rise before your mind's eye, from somewhere out of the depths.[13]

One cannot consciously determine the content of these memories:

Say to yourself, "Now I'm going to remember something from my childhood." Close your eyes and say it. You will remember something totally unexpected. One's will has nothing to do with it. The picture lights up, turned on by some sort of engineers behind your consciousness. (*Ni dnia*, p. 14)

It is characteristic of Olesha to consider a phenomenon which he does not understand as a vast, complex machine,

[13] Literaturnaia tekhnika," p. 429.

controlled by unknown "engineers." But he usually senses the phenomenon of involuntary memory (central, of course, to Proust's works as well) in organic, not mechanical terms. Once more, the vocabulary is one of fluidity. The memory surfaces slowly, rises as through water, gradually emerging.

Once again, Dobrodeev, you surface through the dark expanse of closed centuries. And I still see in that expanse with you the beams of the Stroganovsk bridge. . . . Here you are, running out of your tavern [. . .] (p. 94)

Olesha speaks of what is past as being a "country which no longer exists in space, but is already locked out of space and into time." (p. 291) But time can be unlocked, and the memories which swim to the surface as he writes achieve an almost physical presence in a kind of mental space:

There they are, somersaulting in front of me, there they are—there, right there, is it possible you don't see them? No one sees them! Only I see them, and I see in that nonexistent space that swirls before my eyes and which is called memory. (p. 105)

A sensation can be actually relived in the process of writing it:

That's not something that happened "yesterday" as one always says in such cases; it is literally happening now. I literally see that little table slightly to my left, with its spoon, siphon of seltzer water, sheet of newspaper, a cane, its head buried in a corner of the tablecloth, and those eyes [Maiakovskii's], like those that Homer described as ox's eyes. (pp. 148-49) [. . .] Now I stretch out my hand and the cardboard is in it again and the moment repeats itself! (p. 37)

Furthermore, now that it has been recorded the incident no longer sinks back into the vast undifferentiated emptiness out of which it slowly swam up. The incident or sensation has been fixed.

Thus, writing is the essential element of a complex process which enables Olesha to reconstitute events of his life which had been forgotten, to relive them in terms of sensuous immediacy, and finally to preserve them for himself and for posterity. Olesha cannot remember the earliest period of life, when, he has been told, a baby sees the world upside down. But out of what he can salvage he tries to make a self-created monument, a reconstitution of life in art.

The writing of *No Day* is not only a recording of his life; it is also a redefinition of it. It enables Olesha to try to deal with the complex problem of the relation between the boy who was the initial perceiver and the artist who re-experiences the moment. Olesha tries to decide where the real value lies: in the experiences of life itself or in artistic re-experience—in the moment itself or in the aesthetic impression which crystallizes it. Olesha recalls, for example, returning one evening at dusk from playing soccer. He crossed a patch of small flowers in the grass: "Our feet in their soccer boots trod on them. We simply didn't see them. It's only now, suddenly looking back, that I noticed a whole cloak of flowers—a knightly white cloak, fallen in the grass." (p. 115) It is Olesha the artist who realizes the full poignancy of the moment through the image of the child as a pure and fearless knight unaware that he is walking on the symbol of his election, a symbol as perishable as the innocence it represents.

Sometimes, however, Olesha seems to be saying that the true value is in the original moment:

My grandmother wasn't accompanying a writer but a little boy. He didn't see everything that the writer now remembers. Perhaps it never was at all! No, it was! There's no doubt that it was autumn and the leaves were falling. There's no doubt that they sailed past me, scraping their sides like ships, and like ships they designed a circle, as they sailed around me—two or three twigs spiralled and gently settled on the asphalt, in the gutter where there were already a great many of them, a whole wrecked fleet. Sometimes the breeze turned the prows of some of them in the opposite direction. . . .

No, it was the boy who saw all this. The writer only remembers and enjoys one memory among others. It was the boy who saw. The boy, led by his grandmother. (p. 61)

The problem of the original locus of value is never actually resolved. But in each case the value of the present reliving of the experience is dependent on the written elaboration of the crystallizing metaphor[14]—the knightly white cloak, the complexly structured evocation of swirling leaves. The metaphor itself is the locus of the overcoming of the theoretical dichotomy between time present and past, between life and art. Hence Olesha's insistence on the existential value of the moment of writing in which everything coincides. Then the stirrings of the statue are no longer felt as alien, and Olesha the artist is coextensive both with his past life and with the written work, the making of which creates the momentary synthesis.

Olesha needs to establish the unity of the life he depicts in his fragments. He must cross a void and assert the identity of the boy and the artist so as to be able to reject a third incarnation of himself: the decrepit old man. Unlike Proust, Olesha is unable to finally accept and find a continuity through change, a respect for the old man who is also a part of a life in time. Olesha rejects the old man with hatred. The specter

[14] Cf. Proust: "On peut faire se succéder indéfiniment dans une description les objets qui figuraient dans le lieu décrit, la vérité ne commencera qu'au moment où l'écrivain prendra deux objets différents, posera leur rapport, analogue dans le monde de l'art à celui qu'est le rapport unique de la loi causale dans le monde de la science, et les enfermera dans les anneaux nécessaires d'un beau style; même, ainsi que la vie, quand, en rapprochant une qualité commune à deux sensations, il dégagera leur essence commune en les réunissant l'une à l'autre pour les soustraire aux contingences du temps, dans une métaphore. (*Le Temps retrouvé*, p. 889).

of age has always haunted him,[15] and now that he is almost sixty he is terribly afraid of an increasing lack of sensuous contact with the world. In the formulation of "Liompa," he fears that death in its approach will take the world away and prevent new metaphors from being born within him. By re-experiencing the sensations of an Olesha who has survived unchanged through time, he can reject the physically debilitated old man he sees in the mirror, considering him a mask, the last of a series of doubles which although emanating from an essential self are still indisputably *other*:

> Since nothing happens to the sensation "I'm alive," and it remains the same as when I was a small boy, it is with the same sensation, and as freshly as ever, that I perceive myself to be old; and this old man is terribly new to me—since, I repeat, I might never have lived to see him, and at any rate for many, many years never thought I would. And suddenly an old man looks from the mirror at the young me [. . .] It's fantastic! theatrical! When I move away from the mirror and lie down on the couch, I don't think of myself as being the person I just saw. No, the *I* who lies down is the same *I* who used to lie down when I was a boy. The other one has stayed in the mirror. Now there are two of us—I and he. [. . .]
>
> "Hello, who are you?"
>
> "I'm you."
>
> "No, you're not."
>
> Sometimes I even laugh. The one in the mirror laughs too. I laugh until I cry. And the one in the mirror weeps too. (pp. 171-72)

The world of mirrors has, of course, always been the locus of fantasy for Olesha. But, as we have noted about *Envy*, even when the relations of the world around the beholder were

[15] Cf. such comments as the one in "V mire;" "I am very old . . . despite the fact that I am thirty-one and already notice on myself and in myself signs of physical aging, nonetheless, I have never yet felt as though I were an adult." (p. 339).

distorted, *his* image used to be reflected back unchanged, dominating the rest of the mirror world. Now, however, the very image of the beholder is no longer the same, no longer corresponds to the beholder's own image of himself. Only the special mirror of his art can reflect back the essential Olesha that he wants others to see. Because his boyhood self is still alive in him in the moment of creative synthesis, because he can relive the sensations of this boy through his writing, Olesha can accomplish a switch. He can reject his actual body as if *it* were artificial, and relegate the clown figure, the buffoon, to the realm of "theatricality." The child and the artist fuse in the moment of artistic recreation which exists somewhere out of time, somewhere where the old man, a product of time, does not exist.

No Day without a Line thus provides Olesha with an alternate sphere of existence. It enables him to keep the old man in the mirror at a distance, and thus to disregard the humiliations and weaknesses inflicted on him by an old age that, it is clear from many fragments, he finds almost obscene. The old man, Olesha, taken for just another drunk, is driven away from a bookstall for trying to interfere in a sale: "How theatrical! Could I ever have thought when I was a boy playing soccer, could I ever have thought when I was a famous writer whom a whole theatre used to turn around to look at, that one hot, summer's day I would be chased away from a bookstall—and with reason." (p. 181) The surrounding world, which sees only old Olesha, deprives him not only of his fame but also of his very identity. This is the basic threat. While he is in the hospital, two young nurses who come to take a blood test mispronounce his name, inquiring, "Is Alësha here?" As he watches his blood flow into the little tube, Olesha tries to joke in order to establish some more human contact between himself and them. The girls do not respond: "They see a terrible creature with rheumy eyes, scaly-skinned hands; you are sentenced to death, and they know it. Supple, they get up and go to another bed, and you heave a sigh and almost begin to weep." (p. 168) The girls do not see the Olesha that he considers essential: the famous writer at whom a whole theatre audience stared, making him fully aware of his own existence as an artist by their acknowledgment of it. When others see him only as a decrepit body and are unaware of his fame, it is almost as though the important Olesha, the one whom he wishes to see reflected in the acknowledgment of others, were already dead. In fact, at times, it seems to Olesha that only death is interested in him anymore.

When someone calls out "boy," I look back too. Will I look back now when they call "old man"?

No, I won't look back. Don't I want to? No, the surprising thing is just that it has come so quickly. Can it really have come?

"Old man, hey, old man!"

No, it's not for me, it can't be.

"Old man!"

No, I won't look back. It can't have happened so quickly.

"Old man! What a fool. He won't look around, and it is I, Death, who's calling!" (p. 289)

No Day without a Line is haunted by Olesha's consciousness of the approach of death. For him, time is ultimately measured in terms of the individual life span. Eternity cannot be weighed against the death of one individual, because with each death a whole universe is destroyed. Olesha recalls the first death he ever saw: that of a bandit, lying wounded in the street: "His unique life, the only life given to him in millions, hundreds of millions, billions of years, was ending. I remember that chest, heaving in pain, that whole world, that whole, independent, gigantic universe, perhaps greater than ours, perhaps greater than all the millions of others because it was individual, independent." (p. 129) In the last pages of *No Day* there is a kind of litany: "Today in *Pravda* there was an obituary on the death of Fedor Gladkov." (p. 294) "Aleksandr Vertinskii has died." (p. 296) But if one of the themes that runs through many fragments of *No Day without a Line* is resentment at being fastened to a dying animal, another balancing theme is the certitude of some kind of immortality. Slavin accepts at face value Olesha's assertions that he still believed just as strongly in his physical immortality as he had in his youth,[16] but Slavin disregards an even more characteristic Oleshan statement: that we know nothing of a nonmetaphoric eternity. (p. 257)

Olesha is at least confident that he has achieved the kind of immortality possible through art. He is convinced that "I have written a book, *Envy*, which will live for centuries." (p. 161) Through the greatness of his book, his creative individuality remains alive: "[. . .] we reread great books as though each reading were the first, and that is why their authors have an amazing destiny: they haven't passed away, haven't died. They sit at their desks or stand at their lecterns. They are out of time." (p. 188)

No Day, even if he never finishes it, even if it remains in the form of a diary, will also contribute to his immortality. While it is read, he is alive. Olesha was moved by the diary of Delacroix, which he read during the period when he was working on *No Day without a Line*. What he says of it applies to his own work as well:

When you are reading Delacroix's *Diary*, you feel, palpably, the movement of a physical body beside you. It's not a diary, but life itself restored by the invocation of a mind. Therefore it's all the more terrible to me to notice that I've already read through half the book. He's still writing his entries; even though he's sick, he still thinks, as we all do, that dying is something that can't happen

16 Slavin, *Portrety i zapiski*, p. 26.

to him. . . . But all I have to do is turn over a certain number of pages—and he's already gone, Delacroix, who so loved to eat and paint. (pp. 250-51)

In the same way, Olesha implicitly compares his own fate with that of Tolstoi. In a fragment which begins with an extravagant refusal to consider his own death,[17] Olesha discusses Tolstoi's writings about death, and his physical death at Astapovo. Olesha concludes: "I am thinking about Lev Tolstoi late at night, December 20, 1959." (p. 295) Thus, the creations of an artist who has died[18] and the image of himself left by his own writings and those of people who knew him live on as integral parts of the unique universe of each reader. Olesha's assertions of immortality through art are, of course, banal. But they do mark his final pathetic hope for the successful conclusion of his life-long quest for fame and thus for recognition by others of his existence.

Olesha had declared that metaphor is the part of the writer's art which is immortal, and he turned constantly to metaphors—such as "the artist is a pearl in the maw of time"[19]—to express his hope of immortality. He turned most often to that timeless image of immortality—the sun—to express this poetic aspiration. Light is a sign of grace in Olesha's early works. It remains so in *No Day without a Line*. Indeed, if the sun's light

[17] Olesha died on May 10, 1960, four and a half months after he had written this fragment about Tolstoi, the first lines of which follow: "Still I'm absolutely convinced that I won't die. Despite the fact that people are dying around me—many, many people, both younger than I and my contemporaries—despite the fact that I am old, I don't for a moment admit the thought that I am going to die. Perhaps I actually won't die? Perhaps all this—both life and these deaths—exists in my imagination? Perhaps I am immense, infinite, perhaps I am the Universe." (p. 295)

[18] When Olesha first read *Don Quixote*: "[. . .] the image of a man created by another man entered my consciousness; immortality entered in the form it takes on earth. And I became a fraction of that immortality: I began to think." ("Ia smotriu v proshloe," p. 288)

[19] Lidin, p. 119.

is neoplatonically declared to be the essential element of the material world which "is made of light" (p. 300), the sun itself becomes the ultimate symbol of aspiration. Olesha says, "All my life my gaze has been turned towards the sunset." (p. 180) Elsewhere he declares:

> One walks through the city. . . . It's September, but clean, calm, and warm. And however much one walks, the world doesn't accept one. I have been going somewhere all my life. Nevermind, I'll get there, I thought. Get where? To Paris, Venice, Crakow? No, to the sunset. Even now I walk, although I already know that one can never reach the sunset. Obviously it was a dream about immortality. (p. 301)

The sunset is what can never be reached as one spends a life pursuing it. But the sun is seen not only as something which constantly recedes. It is also important to Olesha as the center of a whole solar system. Perhaps the last fragment of *No Day without a Line* (an extended metaphoric consideration of the poet's relation to the sun seen as the symbolic source of all life and creativity) is the essential text of this book. It begins as a typically delicate Oleshan description of birches:

> Some of them are very tall, voluminous. White trunk, transparent, bright foliage. The black crosscuts on the bark of the trunk looked like steamships, hatchets, figures from diagrams. Tiny siskins perched among the foliage, very small and green, looking like leaves. One on a hillock looked at me like a woman who had drawn the edge of her shawl about her face. . . .
>
> I must write a book about saying farewell to the world.
>
> Very often I go for very long walks alone. And nonetheless my link with some sort of power plant or other remains unbroken. Does that mean that I live entirely within myself? How is that possible? Can it be that I carry within myself all life's energy? Can the whole conductor be in me, the whole battery? Can it be that all my life is myself? That I am my whole life? That's not possible.

It's obvious an external environment has been controlling me at every step of the way since I came into the world. Obviously the sun has had me on a wire, on a string, all the time, and has moved me, and is the power plant which constantly charges me.

It shows through the thin but almost impenetrable barrier of clouds as a turbidly shining circle—it barely penetrates, and still the shadows are visible on the stone. It is barely discernible, but still I can see my shadow on the sidewalk as well as the shadow of the gates and, most important, even the shadow of some spring catkins, dangling from a tree.

What is the sun? Nothing in my human life would have taken place without the participation of the sun--both actual and hidden, both real and metaphoric. Whatever I have done, wherever I have gone, whether dreaming or awake, in darkness, young or old, I have always been at the end of a sunbeam. (p. 303)

Of course the poet, child of the sun, always at the end of his own particular sunbeam, is a typically romantic image. But the importance of the passage is not so much that it is a statement of poetic election. It is also an admission of dependence on some external force—an admission which enables Olesha to integrate himself into a system, to subordinate himself metaphorically to something which may be perceived as objectively eternal. Olesha has overcome fragmentation and isolation. He has achieved wholeness by realizing that he is a part of the most perfect and symmetrical of systems. Because he feels secure in his relationship to the ultimate source of all life and power, he no longer needs to see himself as the radial center. He is content to be tied to it and illumined by a single beam of light, once and for all accepting a passive, feminine role. He is satisfied to see himself as a part of a whole rather than trying to contain everything within himself. The passage is therefore a statement of confidence in the structure of the universe beyond him, a recognition of proportion based on his conviction that his "unique nonrepeatable I" will not be totally destroyed, but will be preserved in the only kind of immortality he knows is possible, immortality through art.

Thus, after an artistic career which began as an attempt to impose an idiosyncratic vision upon the world, to pervert its relations, subjecting it to the shaping control of the artist's individual consciousness—and thereby to impose himself on the world—Olesha feels that his mark has been made. He can now celebrate an independently existing world. He has come to the point where he can declare, "Hurrah for everything that lives, in the grass, in caves, among the rocks. Hurrah for the world without me!" (p. 272) He feels that his art has finally "embraced his life like the sky."

Conclusion

In a moment of despair, Olesha once declared, "Just wait! I'll die and *then* I'll live!"[1] Although during his lifetime Olesha felt deprived of fame, in the years since his death memoirs by Lev Slavin, Vladimir Lidin, Emmanuel Kazakevich, Konstantin Paustovskii, and Viktor Shklovskii have begun to fold around Olesha a kind of posthumous legend. Slavin attributes charisma to him:

Even while he was still alive, the aura of legend began to gather around Olesha. [. . .] Many people became satellites in constant orbit around him. That was the effect of his talent, and in his best moments Olesha had real greatness. But he didn't realize it, and envied the fame of Dumas-père, a writer he despised.[2]

Olesha was, therefore, as he had always aspired to be, a sun, the focus of the attention of others.

Everyone who reminisces about Olesha emphasizes his brilliance as an improviser and performer. At a moment's notice he could produce splendid images for an audience which watched fascinated as he shaped and controlled his material before their eyes. Although the product of a far longer and more deliberate effort, *Envy* itself partakes of the quality of a marvelous improvisation. A tour de force, it keeps the reader in constant amazement before the artist's seemingly inexhaustible invention.

[1] *Ni dnia*, p. 12.
[2] Slavin, *Portrety i zapiski*, pp. 14-15.

It is only just that Olesha should be remembered as a performer. His first dreams of fame and aesthetic control were determined by the graceful movements of circus artists. To be at the center of attention and be seen by thousands in the flawless accomplishment of feats of agility, to evoke admiration, even love, in the hearts of those who were the spectators of his prowess was Olesha's continuing desire. Olesha's image of the artist was therefore primarily that of the performing artist, the entertainer.

This is not to minimize the importance of the artist. His improvisations and transformations of the world were destined to fill the leisure hours of the new socialist man. The capacity for amazement and a taste for the play of imagination were, in Olesha's view, essential elements of any truly human being. By helping to develop these faculties, Olesha's art would participate in the construction of Communism.

He would not, however, have it serve in any other way. As we saw in "The Cherry Stone," Olesha thought of his art as complementary to the Five-Year Plan, but of an entirely different nature from it. Art would be a tree in the garden, a focus of delighted attention within the protective curve of the concrete colossus of socialism.

Our sympathies are all with Olesha when he thus exempts his art from the menial tasks of exhortation and agitprop. But approval of his refusal to debase art to the level of immediate social command may prevent us from realizing the full extent of Olesha's evasions. Olesha was unwilling to take the responsibility of regarding his art as anything but diversion. If the artist is an entertainer, he is outside the pale of constricting, adult, utilitarian categories. He is not responsible. He therefore cannot be guilty.

As we have seen in "The Prophet," to demand solid results from imagination is to run the risk of moral failure. Only the writer who refuses to "stretch his own soul over the abyss as a tightrope and to totter upon it"[3] is sure not to fall and destroy himself. Maiakovskii's soul snapped under the weight of the poetic responsibility he had assumed. Olesha refused to venture this. In fact, despite the seeming daring of such works as *Envy*, its apparently destructive and disintegrating perception of the world, Olesha's fundamental attitude was not one of boldness, but of caution.

Olesha was the victim of an odd lucidity in both political and artistic realms. If he was incapable of accommodating himself to the imperfection of the world, he nonetheless could not commit himself to a political extreme. He feared action, knowing that it destroys as it builds. "Everything must change," says Olesha. But when change had come, he, like his heroine Goncharova, was paralyzed by his recognition of the justice of the Revolution, unwilling to declare against it, yet unable to devote himself wholeheartedly to it because of the things he loved which the Revolution could not but destroy.

We have seen in the preceding pages how Olesha refuses to commit himself even to his own images, how he undercuts his metaphors, how he vanquishes his false prophets. Even Kavalerov is no Don Quixote, breaking his heart, vainly tilting at windmills in the conviction that they are giants. Kavalerov pretends he is fighting giants because he knows that they are really windmills.

In fact, Olesha refuses to allow the rationality of his heroes to be completely destroyed by anything short of death. He will not commit them to the disintegration of insanity. His imagination spends itself in finding ways to deal with the incomprehensible and to avoid the uncontrollable. That is why Olesha himself declares, "Fancy is the Beloved of Reason."[4]

Olesha thus finally refuses to commit himself not only to the new world around him but also even to the power of his own

[3] Maiakovskii, "Fleita-pozvonochnik," part 3, lines 343-5.

[4] *Zavist'*, p. 77.

imagination. Commitment means that one is no longer free to retreat and must accept the possibility of self-sacrifice or destruction. We have seen that the brilliant products of Olesha's fantasy are part of a lifelong attempt to protect himself against such destruction. Unlike a constraining uniform imposed on him by others, his works form an armor of his own choosing. The are a bright, protective coating in which Olesha confronts the world and forces it to see him as he wishes to be seen, while convincing himself of his own safety. At the center of Olesha's creativity was the consciousness of his own softness and vulnerability. Around the first, irritating grain of fear there formed, by a slow and often painful process, layers of protective secretion, the self-created image of the artist Iurii Olesha, a small but glittering "pearl in the maw of time."

A Selected Bibliography

Aksenov, Vasilii. *Pora, moi drug, pora.* Moscow, Molodaia gvardiia, 1965.

Babitsky, Paul,* and John Rimberg. *The Soviet Film Industry.* New York, Frederick A. Praeger, 1955.

Bachelard, Gaston. *L'Air et les songes.* Paris, Librairie José Corti, 1943.

———. *La Poétique de l'espace.* Paris, Presses Universitaires de France, 1957.

Bachelis, I. "Nash otvet poputchiku Zandu," *30 dnei,* No. 1 (1932), pp. 18-20.

Badikov, V. V. "Nabliudenie nad iazykom i stilem Iuriia Oleshi," *Filologicheskii sbornik* (Alma-Alta), No. 3 (1964).

———. "O stile romana Iuriia Oleshi *Zavist',*" *Filologicheskii sbornik* (Alma Alta), No. 4 (1964), pp. 54-62.

Béguin, Albert. *L'Ame romantique et le rêve.* Paris, Librairie José Corti, 1946.

Belyi, Andrei. "Magiia slov," in *Simvolizm.* Moscow, 1910.

Berkovskii, N. "O prozaikakh," *Zvezda,* No. 12 (1929), pp. 147-56 [portion on Olesha, pp. 149-54].

———. *Tekushchaia literatura.* Moscow, Izdatel'stvo "Federatsiia," 1930.

Brainina, B. *Konstantin Fedin.* Moscow, Sovetskii Pisatel', 1951.

Brik, Osip. "Simuliatsiia nevmeniaemosti," *Novyi Lef,* No. 7, (1928), pp. 1-3.

Brown, Edward J. *Russian Literature Since the Revolution.* New York, Collier Books, 1963.

* For the reader's convenience, the author's name has been given in the transliteration which appears on the title page of his book.

Cherbotarevskaia, T. "Tibul izmenil Iu. Oleshe," *Literaturnaia gazeta*, Dec. 24, 1966.

Cherniak, Ia. "O *Zavisti* Iuriia Oleshi," *Pechat' i revoliutsiia*, No. 5 (1928), pp. 107-12.

Chudakova, M. "Poetika Iuriia Oleshi," *Voprosy literatury*, No. 4 (1968), pp. 120-31.

El'sberg, Zh. *Krizis poputchikov i nastroeniia intelligentsii*. Moscow, Priboi, 1930.

Erenburg, Il'ia. *Neobychainye pokhozhdeniia Khulio Khurenito i ego uchenikov*. Moscow-Berlin, Izdatel'stvo "Gelikon," 1922.

———. *V Protochnom pereulke* in *Sobranie sochinenii v deviati tomakh*. II. Moscow, Izdatel'stvo "Khudozhestvennaia literatura," 1964.

Ershov, L. F. *Sovetskaia satiricheskaia proza*. Moscow-Leningrad, Izdat. Akademii nauk SSSR, 1960.

Ershov, Petr. "Odesskaia literaturnaia kolybel'," *Opyty* (New York), No. 8 (1957), pp. 93-99.

Fedin, Konstantin. *Brat'ia*. Moscow, Sovetskii Pisatel', 1948.

———. *Goroda i gody* in *Sobranie sochinenii v deviati tomakh*. II. Moscow, Gosudarstvennoe izdatel'stvo khudozhestvennoi literatury, 1959.

Frid, A. Review of *L'Ecole des indifférents* in *Pechat' i revoliutsiia*, No. 1 (1928), pp. 194-96.

Frioux, Claude. "Sur deux romans d'Aleksandr Grin," *Cahiers du Monde Russe et Soviétique*, No. 4 (Oct.-Dec., 1962), pp. 546-63.

Giraudoux, Jean. *L'Ecole des indifférents*. Paris, Bernard Grasset, 1922.

Golubov, V. "Spisok blagodeianii," *Rabochii i teatr*, No. 28 (Oct. 1931), p. 5.

Gorbov, D. "Opravdanie *Zavisti*," *Novyi mir*, No. 11 (1928), pp. 218-30.

Gorbov, D. "V zashchitu literatury," *Pechat' i revoliutsiia*, No. 8 (1928), pp. 96-106.

Grin, Aleksandr. *Izbrannoe*, with an introductory article "Zhizn' Aleksandra Grina," by Konstantin Paustovskii. Moscow, Gosudarstvennoe izdatel'stvo khudozhestvennoi literatury, 1956.

———. *Sobranie sochinenii v shesti tomakh*, with an introductory article "Rytsar' mechty," by V. Vikhrov. Moscow, Biblioteka "Ogonek," Izdatel'stvo "Pravda," 1965.

———. *Zolotaia tsep'* and *Doroga nikuda,* with a postface "V chem volshebstvo Aleksandra Grina?" by Vl. Dmitrevskii. Leningrad, Gosudarstvennoe izdatel'stvo detskoi literatury, 1960.

Grossman-Roshchin, I. "Iskusstvo izmeniat' mir," *Na literaturnom postu,* No. 1 (Jan., 1929), pp. 20-25; No. 4-5 (Feb.-March, 1929), pp. 28-34; No. 8 (April, 1929), pp. 4-17.

Gurvich, Aleksandr. *Tri dramaturga.* Moscow, Goslitizdat, 1936.

———. *V poiskakh geroia.* Moscow-Leningrad, Gosudarstvennoe izdatel'stvo, 1938.

Harkins, William. "The Philosophical Tales of Jurij Oleša," in *Orbis Scriptus: Dmitrij Tschižewskij zum 70. Geburtstag.* Edited by Dietrich Gerhardt et al. Munich, Wilhelm Fink Verlag, 1966, pp. 349-54.

———. "The Theme of Sterility in Olesha's *Envy,*" *Slavic Review,* No. 3 (September, 1966), pp. 444-57.

Huxley, Aldous. *The Doors of Perception.* Harmondsworth, Penguin Books, 1959.

———. *Heaven and Hell.* Harmondsworth, Penguin Books, 1959.

Iakobson, Roman. *Noveishaia russkaia poeziia.* Prague, 1921.

Jackson, Robert L. *Dostoevsky's Underground Man in Russian Literature.* The Hague, Mouton & Co., 1958.

Jelagin, Juri.* *Taming of the Arts.* New York, E. P. Dutton and Co., Inc., 1951.

Kataev, Valentin. "Proshchanie s mirom," *Znamia,* No. 3 (1966), pp. 249-50.

Katanian, V. *Maiakovskii, literaturnaia khronika.* 4th rev. ed. Moscow, Gosudarstvennoe izdatel'stvo khudozhestvennoi literatury, 1961.

Kaverin, Veniamin. *Khudozhnik neizvesten* in *Sobranie sochinenii v shesti tomakh.* II. Moscow, Izdatel'stvo "Khudozhestvennaia literatura," 1964.

* For the reader's convenience, the author's name has been given in the transliteration which appears on the title page of his book.

———. *Khudozhnik neizvesten* in *Zvezda,* No. 8 (1931), pp. 5-82 [original, uncut version].

———. "Pisateli o meshchanstve," *Na literaturnom postu,* No. 6 (March, 1929), p. 24.

———. *Vorob'inaia noch'*. Moscow, Artel' pisatelei "Krug," 1927.

Kayser, Wolfgang. *The Grotesque in Art and Literature.* Translated by Ulrich Weisstein. Bloomington, Indiana University Press, 1963.

Kirpotin, Valerii. *Proza, dramaturgiia i teatr.* Moscow, Gosudarstvennoe izdatel'stvo "Khudozhestvennaia literatura," 1935.

Kruchonykh, A., and V. Khlebnikov. *Slovo kak takovoe.* Moscow, 1913.

Lauer, Reinhard. "Zur Gestalt Ivan Babičevs in Olešas *Zavist'*," *Die Welt der Slaven,* VII (1962), 45-54.

Leonov, Leonid. *Doroga na okean.* Moscow, Izdatel'stvo Sovetskaia Rossiia, 1961.

Levin, Lev. *Na znakomye temy.* Leningrad, Gosudarstvennoe izdatel'stvo "Khudozhestvennaia literatura," 1937.

Lezhnev, A., and D. Gorbov. *Literatura revoliutsionnogo desiatiletiia.* Moscow, Izdatel'stvo proletarii, 1929.

Lezhnev, A. *Literaturnye budni.* Moscow, Izdatel'stvo "Federatsiia," 1929.

———. "O molodykh pisateliakh," *Pechat' i revoliutsiia,* No. 2-3 (1929), pp. 77-91.

Libedinskaia, Lidia. *Zelenaia lampa.* Moscow, Sovetskii Pisatel', 1966.

Libedinskii, Iu. "Segodnia poputnicheskoi literatury i zadachi LAPP," *Zvezda,* No. 1 (1930), pp. 177-90.

Lidin, Vladimir. *Liudi i vstrechi.* Moscow, Sovetskii Pisatel', 1961.

Maiakovskii, Vladimir. *The Bedbug and Selected Poetry.* Translated by Max Hayward and George Reavey, edited by Patricia Blake. New York, Meridian Books, 1960.

———. "Vladimir Maiakovskii—Tragediia," in *Sobranie sochinenii v chetyrekh tomakh.* I. Moscow, Gosudarstvennoe izdatel'stvo "Khudozhestvennaia literatura," 1936.

Marx, Karl, and Friedrich Engels. *Literature and Art; Selections from their Writings.* New York, International Publishers, 1947.

———. *Sur la littérature et l'art.* Edited by Jean Fréville. Paris, Editions Sociales Internationales, 1936.

Mathewson, Rufus W., Jr. *The Positive Hero in Russian Literature.* New York, Columbia University Press, 1958.

Meierkhol'd, Vsevolod. "Spisok blagodeianii," in *Stat'i, pis'ma, rechi, besedy, 1917-39.* Moscow, Izdatel'stvo "Iskusstvo," 1968. pp. 249-54.

Meilakh, B. "Zapiski vliublennogo v zhizn'," *Neva,* No. 9 (1965), pp. 193-94.

Moiseev, Igor A. *Tri tolstiaka* [Ballet adaptation of Iurii Olesha's *Tri tolstiaka*]. Moscow, Gosudarstvennyi akademecheskii bol'shoi teatr SSR Armenii, 1935.

Nabokov, Vladimir. *Dar.* New York, Chekhov Press, 1952.

———. *The Eye.* New York, Pocket Books, 1966.

Nikolaev, Ia. "Iurii Olesha—*Tri tolstiaka,*" *Na literaturnom postu,* No. 4-5 (1929), p. 108.

Nikulin, Lev. "Eshche o Iurii Oleshe," *Moskva,* No. 9 (1965), pp. 213-15.

———. *Gody nashei zhizni.* Moscow, Moskovskii Rabochii, 1966.

Nilsson, Nils Ake. "Through the Wrong End of Binoculars," *Scando-Slavica,* XI (1965), 40-68.

Novitskii, Pavel. "O kulturnoi zrelosti sovetskogo teatra," *Pechat' i revoliutsiia,* No. 4 (1929), pp. 97-108.

Olesha, Iurii, "At Work on a Play," *Soviet Travel,* No. 3 (1934), pp. 25-26, 29, 77.

———. "Chernyi chelovek," *30 dnei,* No. 6 (1932), pp. 27-31 [not the complete play].

———. Statement in "Discussia o porche iazyka," *Na literaturnom postu,* No. 11-12 (1929), pp. 69-73 [Olesha's statement, p. 71].

———. "Divano-krovat'," *Krokodil,* No. 23 (1934), p. 10. Signed, Iurii Karlov.

———. "Gnat' iz teatra khalturu," *Literaturnaia gazeta,* January 24, 1931.

———. "Gost'," *Ogonek,* No. 31 (1937), p. 13.

———. "Igra v plakhu," *30 dnei,* No. 5 (1934), pp. 35-48.

———. "Iurii Olesha Talks with His Readers," *International Literature,* No. 3 (1936), pp. 77-88.

———. *Izbrannoe.* Moscow, Gosudarstvennoe izdatel'stvo "Khudozhestvennaia literatura," 1935.

———. *Izbrannye sochineniia,* with an introduction by V. Pertsov. Moscow, Gosudarstvennoe izdatel'stvo khudozhestvennoi literatury, 1956.

———. "Iz literaturnykh dnevnikov," *Literaturnaia Moskva.* II. Moscow. Gosudarstvennoe izdatel'stvo khudozhestvennoi literatury, 1956, pp. 721-51.

———. Statement in "Khronika—pisateli o sebe," *Na literaturnom postu,* No. 4-5 (1929), p. 120.

———. "Koe-chto iz sekretnykh zapisei poputchika Zanda," *30 dnei,* No. 1 (1932), pp. 11-17.

———. "Literatura—obshchee delo pisatelia i rabochego," *Literaturnaia gazeta,* December 17, 1933.

———. "Meyerhold: Soviet Director on His Sixtieth Birthday," *International Literature,* No. 2 (June, 1934), pp. 137-138.

———. "Nasha rodina," *30 dnei,* No. 4 (1938), pp. 7-8.

———. "Neobkhodimost' perestroiki mne iasna: otvet Iuriia Oleshi litkruzhku Dvoretsstroia," *30 dnei,* No. 5 (1932), pp. 67-68.

———. *Ni dnia bez strochki,* with an introduction by Viktor Shklovskii. Moscow, Izdatel'stvo "Sovetskaia Rossiia," 1965.

———. "Ni dnia bez stroki," [*sic*] *Oktiabr',* No. 7 (1961), pp. 147-69; No. 8 (1961), pp. 135-56, with an introduction by Viktor Shklovskii.

———. "Noch'," *30 dnei,* No. 4 (1937), pp. 15-23. [Extracts from the scenario *Val'ter.* A. Macheret was co-author.]

———. "Notes of a Writer," *International Literature,* No. 3 (July, 1934), pp. 148-151.

———. "O malenkikh p'esakh," *30 dnei,* No. 8 (1933), pp. 64-65.

———. *P'esy.* with an introductory article by P. Markov. Moscow, Izdatel'stvo "Iskusstvo," 1968.

———. "Pisateli o meshchanstve," *Na literaturnom postu,* No. 6 (March, 1929), p. 28.

———. "Pis'mo pisateliu Paustovskomu," *Literaturnaia gazeta,* August, 26, 1937.

———. *Povesti i rasskazy,* with an introduction "Mir Oleshi," by

B. Galanov. Moscow, Izdatel'stvo "Khudozhestvennaia Literatura," 1965.
———. "Smert' Zanda," *Literaturnaia gazeta,* October 19, 1930.
———. Speech in *Sovetskaia literatura na novom etape* [the stenographic report of the first plenum of the organizing committee of the Union of Soviet Writers, October 29-November 3, 1932]. Moscow, 1933.
———. *Spisok blagodeianii.* Berlin-Charlottenburg, Izdatel'stvo "Kniga i stsena," 1931.
———. "Stena uchenykh," *Ogonek,* No. 32 (1947), p. 23.
———. Introduction to the Moiseev adaptation of *Tri tolstiaka, see* Moiseev.
———. *The Wayward Comrade and the Commissars.* Translated by Andrew MacAndrew. New York, Signet, 1960. [A translation of *Zavist'* and several short stories.]
———. "Zagovor chuvstv," *Oktiabr',* No. 1 (January, 1929), pp. 33-50 [selected scenes].
———. "Zakaz na strashnoe," *30 dnei,* No. 2 (1936), pp. 33-36.
———. "Zametki o literature," *30 dnei,* No. 3 (1937), pp. 87-90.
———. "Zametki pisatel'ia," *Literaturnyi kritik,* No. 1 (1934), pp. 180-85 [not the same as the *International Literature* text with the same English title].
———. "Za tri dnia," *30 dnei,* No. 6 (1936), pp. 31-34.
———. "Zerkal'tse," *Ogonek,* No. 1 (January 6, 1946), p. 9.
———. The poems of "Zubilo." *Passim* in *Gudok* (1921-1922).
Ol'khovyi, B. "Esche raz o literaturnom poputnichestve," *Pechat' i revoliutsiia,* No. 8 (1929), pp. 12-28.
———. "O poputnichestve i poputnikakh," *Pechat' i revoliutsiia,* No. 5 (1929), pp. 3-18; No. 6 (1929), pp. 3-22.
Ostrovskii, Iu. "Problema intelligentsii v tvorchestve Iuriia Oleshi," *Literaturnyi kritik,* No. 2 (February, 1934), pp. 8-28.
"Otkrytoe pis'mo rabochego litkruzhka Dvoretsstroia pisateliu Iuriiu Oleshe," *30 dnei,* No. 3 (1932), pp. 63-64.
Oulanoff, Hongor. *The Serapion Brothers.* The Hague, Mouton & Co., 1966.
"Pamiati Iuriia Oleshi," *Literaturnaia gazeta,* May 12, 1960.

Papernie, E. *Poeticheskii obraz u Maiakovskogo.* Moscow, Izdat. Akademii nauk SSSR, 1961.

Paustovskii, Konstantin. "Vstrechi s Oleshei," in *Tarruskie stranitsy.* Edited by V. Koblinkov et al. Kaluga, Kaluzhskoe knizhnoe izdatel'stvo, 1961, pp. 34-36.

Pertsov, Viktor. "Lichnost' i sotsialisticheskoe delo," *Oktiabr',* No. 7 (1937), pp. 175-84.

Pesis, Boris. "Pisatel'skie nastroeniia sovremennoi Frantsii," *Pechat' i revoliutsiia,* No. 4 (1927), pp. 5-22.

Polonskii, V. "Ocherki sovremennoi literatury (preodolenie *Zavisti*)," *Novyi mir,* No. 5 (May, 1929), pp. 189-208.

Proffer, Carl. "Notes on the Imagery in Zamjatin's *We,*" *Slavic and East European Journal,* No. 3 (Fall, 1963), pp. 269-78.

Proust, Marcel. *Le Temps Retrouvé,* in *A la Recherche du temps perdu.* Paris, Gallimard, Bibliothèque de la Pléiade, © 1954.

Reeve, F. D. *The Russian Novel.* New York, McGraw-Hill, 1966.

Richards, I. A. *The Philosophy of Rhetoric.* London, Oxford University Press, 1936.

Ripellino, Angelo Maria. *Maiakovski et le théâtre russe d'avant-garde.* Paris, L'Arche, 1965.

Rozanova, E. I. "O romane-skazke Iuriia Oleshi *Tri tolstiaka,*" *Voprosy russkoi literatury,* No. 4 (1967), pp. 82-88.

Russkie sovetskie pisateli—prozaiki. III. Leningrad, 1964, 348-67.

Selivanovskii, A. "Kovarstvo i liubov' Zanda," *Literaturnaia gazeta,* February 29, 1932.

———. "O sotsializme i drevonasazhdenii," an open letter to Olesha in *Literaturnaia gazeta,* June 30, 1931.

Severin, Ev. "Veniamin Kaverin," *Pechat' i revoliutsiia,* No. 1 (1929), pp. 83-90.

Shane, Alex M. *The Life and Works of Evgenij Zamjatin.* Berkeley, University of California Press, 1968.

Shattuck, Roger. *Proust's Binoculars.* New York, Vintage Books, 1967.

Shklovskii, Viktor. "Mir bez glubiny," *Literaturnyi kritik,* No. 5 (October, 1933), pp. 118-21.

———. "O prostote," *Literaturnaia gazeta,* June 5, 1933.

———. *O teorii prozy.* Moscow, Izdatel'stvo "Federatsiia," 1929.

———. *Zoo: pis'ma ne o liubvi, ili tret'ia Eloiza.* Berlin, "Gelikon," 1923.

Simmons, Ernest. *Russian Fiction and Soviet Ideology.* New York, Columbia University Press, 1958.

Slavin, Lev. *Portrety i zapiski.* Moscow, Sovetskii Pisatel', 1965.

Sobolev, Vl. "Guliaia v sadu," *Literaturnaia gazeta,* May 29, 1933 [an interview with Olesha].

———. "Izgnanie metafori," interview with V. Kataev in *Literaturnaia gazeta,* May 17, 1933.

Stahlberger, Lawrence L. *The Symbolic System of Majakovskij.* The Hague, Mouton & Co., 1964.

Stilman, Leon. "Nabliudeniia nad nekotorymi osobennostiami kompozitsii i stilia v romane Tolstogo *Voina i mir,*" *American Contributions to the Fifth International Congress of Slavists—Sofia, 1963.* The Hague, Mouton & Co., 1963, pp. 327-70.

Struve, Gleb. "Pisatel' nenuzhnykh tem (Tvorcheskaia sud'ba Iuriia Oleshi)," *Novyi zhurnal,* XXV (New York, 1951), 139-58.

———. *Soviet Russian Literature 1917-1950.* Norman, University of Oklahoma Press, 1951.

Timofeev, L. I. *Kratkii slovar literaturovedecheskikh terminov.* Moscow, 1952.

Tkhorzhevskii, Ivan. *Russkaia literatura.* Paris, Izdatel'stvo "Vozrozhdenie," 1946.

Toman, John. "Iurii Olesha: Soviet Criticism of his Thought and Literary Expression." Unpublished Columbia University Russian Institute Master's Essay, 1958.

Toporov, A. *Krest'iane o pisateliakh.* Moscow and Leningrad, Gosizdat., 1930.

Urban, A. "Ot metaphory k romanu." Review of *Ni dnia bez strochki* in *Zvezda,* No. 10 (1965), pp. 211-13.

Van Der Eng-Liedmeier, A. M. *Soviet Literary Characters.* The Hague, Mouton & Co., 1959.

Vinogradov, Viktor. *Stilistika, Teoriia poeticheskoi rechi, Poetika.* Moscow, Izdat. Akademii nauk SSSR, 1963.

Vladimirov, S., and D. Zolotnitskii (eds.). *Ocherki istorii russkoi sovetskoi dramaturgii 1917-34.* Leningrad-Moscow, Izdatel'stvo Iskusstvo, 1963. Article on Olesha by L. Klimova, pp. 294-305.

Wells, H. G. "The Door in the Wall," in *The Country of the Blind.* London, Thomas Nelson & Sons, n.d.

Zamiatin, Evgenii. *My.* New York, Izdatel'stvo imeni Chekhova, 1952.

Zavalishin, V. *Early Soviet Writers.* New York, Frederick A. Praeger, c. 1958.

Zelinskii, Kornelii. *Kriticheskie pis'ma.* Moscow, Izdatel'stvo "Federatsiia," 1932.

Index